COURAGE

and

RESILIENCE

ONE MAN'S STORY

By

KEVIN HUGHES BM OAM

2025

To order additional copy of this book, contact:
2708 Armidale Road Blaxland's Creek
New South Wales 2460 Australia
info@shrubspublishing.com

"Courage is not the absence of fear, but the triumph over it. The brave man is not he who does not feel afraid, but he who conquers that fear."

Nelson Mandela

"Have the courage to act instead of react."

Oliver Wendell Holmes

"Courage conquers all things: it even gives strength to the body."

Ovid

"Courage is not having the strength to go on; it is going on when you don't have the strength."

Teddy Roosevelt

ACKNOWLEDGEMENTS

Thanks to my wife Debrena for her constant love and support. You are an amazing human being.

Thanks to M E Skeel for her help to edit my writings.

DEDICATION

This book is for all First Responders around the world and especially to our Coalition Forces within Australia and overseas fighting against terror to make our world a safer place.

CONTENTS

Prologue

As a child, he climbed to a rooftop to be closer to the sky and dream of flying. He had no fear because he didn't yet know how much hurt comes with falling.

Eager to prove himself, he learned a trade. Hungry for excitement, he drove fast cars, played rough and tumble footy and fell in love for the first time.

Love failed and he moved on. Seeking adventure, he joined the Armed Forces and trained as a firefighter. There, and as a civilian fire fighter and first responder, he learned that he could run into the fire, but he couldn't save everyone. The failures haunted him in new dreams that became nightmares.

He saved his money to pay for flying lessons. He became part of the Coast Watch – an Outback Pilot flying missions all over the Northern Territory and Far North Queensland.

On the weekends he took sky divers up and away. When a skydiver became entangled under the plane, he risked his life to save her. The aerial rescue was so daring that it earned him a medal and he came to the attention of influential men.

They offered him a job in espionage, and he became a ghost – a seemingly non-existent pilot flying an invisible plane that all denied existed. The missions he flew tested him in ways he had never imagined before.

When enough was enough he came home and found love. But the nightmares continued… And at last, he had to confront them.

Chapter 1

Reaching for the Sky

I was born in 1957. The Australia of my childhood was a vastly different place to the Australia of today. When I was born, the Prime Minister was Robert Menzies and life moved at a slower pace. Firecrackers were legal, and people stood for God Save the Queen when they went to the movies. TV was black and white, and Australia's favourite show was Pick a Box. Space travel was just starting, planes were still mostly propellor driven, and the British were exploding nuclear weapons at Maralinga.

I was raised in a small dwelling in Toowong before moving to a high set Queenslander with a very high-pitched corrugated roof.

When I was 3 years old, my father left a timber ladder leaning against the back of the house. I went outside to play and discovered it. I remembered seeing my father climbing the ladder, so I decided to try it. I scrambled up like a little monkey. It wasn't hard at all, and I felt no fear. It just seemed to come naturally.

After reaching the roof, I could see that I could go higher to the very top of the roof. So, I climbed off the ladder and crawled to the top. I looked out and thought I was up in the sky with all the aircraft looking down onto the cars and people below.

Then I heard my mother screaming as my father came running. All I remember is him shouting: 'Don't move, son, don't move.'

My father climbed the ladder and scrambled up the steep roof to rescue me. After he got me down, my mother asked me what I had been doing.

I told her that 'I was flying with the planes and the people in them.' I'm sure my mother's first grey hairs appeared that day! But I was meant to be a daredevil and my hunger for adventure was full on. Most of all, I wanted to fly.

I am an only child as my mother lost one of her kidneys after my birth. She never recovered from that operation, and she suffered all kinds of medical issues throughout her life. My father was a fabulous husband, one of the best I have ever known and I'm very proud to call him my father. My parents were simple people and never asked for anything.

They met one day outside of Proud's jewellers in Brisbane. Dad was a worker at the abattoir and Mum was a bookkeeper. They fell in love at first sight and never looked back. They were inseparable. My father never complained about anything. If he was sick, you never knew. He looked after my mother till the day he died.

Dad and Mum

My fathers' parents were Colin and Ethel Hughes. My grandfather Colin was a builder and later became a champion racehorse trainer based at Eagle Farm racecourse in Brisbane.

My mother's parents were Thomas and Mable Denovan. She was the youngest of their five children. My grandfather was Scottish, and my grandmother was born just north of London. They met on a ship coming from Southampton to Melbourne in the early 1930's and married in Melbourne. Then they moved to Brisbane not long after.

I remember fondly the times I spent with them. My grandfather was a telephone technician in Scotland but when he moved to Australia, he became a gas fitter and repaired combustion stoves under his high set house. Their daughter, my aunt Stella, moved into a house across the road from them after she married. That house was right under the flight path of the arriving and departing aircraft from the old Eagle Farm airport. I stood out on the porch for hours watching the aircraft come and go.

From that porch I witnessed the first 747 Jumbo land at Eagle Farm and the flyover of G for George, the Lancaster aircraft on route from England and now in the War Memorial in Canberra. That small deck at the top of the front stairs held great memories for me. I could see for miles on a clear day. Auntie Stella's two children were Peter and Pam. Peter always teased me about the ghosts that lived up near the TV towers and told me that if I walked out onto the deck of a night they would come and get me. Pam, on the other hand, was a very gentle and caring soul who always looked after me.

My uncle Arthur never married. He joined Brisbane's main newspaper, the Courier Mail, as a junior and later moved over to the ABC television network where he worked in the sporting department. He appeared nightly on the news channel reporting on all the sport in Queensland. He became head commentator for the ABC at Lang Park, calling the Sunday football. He travelled the world with the ABC and was their national commentator along with Norman May for the swimming at the National Empire Games (now the Commonwealth Games) held in Perth Australia in 1962. From then on, he appeared at every Olympic and Commonwealth Games until he retired in 1994.

While I was based at Kingswood Bomb Depot with the RAAF west of Sydney, I returned home to visit my parents now and then on weekends. I would always try and visit my uncle's place. In 1982, through Uncle Arthur's contacts at the Brisbane Commonwealth Games, I got to meet a host of world class athletes, including Raelene Boyle, Lisa Curry, Glynis Nunn, Keith Poole, Lisa Forrest, Michelle Ford, Jon Sieben and Neil Brooks. I felt incredibly lucky!

My Aunt Hilda married the manager of a 5000 acre property out near Wandoan north of Miles in Queensland. My parents allowed me to visit on school holidays. I remember catching the McCafferty's bus service from Brisbane to Miles where my aunty and uncle picked me up. Uncle Bill was a tough but fair man. He came from the land. He used to take me kangaroo shooting in places where their numbers were too high. I was taught how to ride a horse and drive the tractors. It was a memorable time in my life. Their two children Brian and Faye were wonderful cousins. Faye became a nursing sister, and Brian joined the Royal Australian Army.

I turned three in 1960. This was a decade that saw many changes, but Menzies was still Prime Minister. The Reserve bank and the Commonwealth bank were created, oral contraceptives came out, the Parkes radio telescope was opened and assisted in the moon landing. Indigenous Australians were recognized as citizens and given the right to vote. The RAAF bought its first Mirage fighter jets, the Beatles toured Australia, Australians fought in Vietnam and National Service was reintroduced. The Americans established a spy base at Pine Gap and the country went metric, abandoning pounds and pence, feet and inches forever.

My father joined the Royal Australian Air Force in 1961, and I clearly remember the day he left from the South Brisbane Railway Station. I cried and cried and couldn't understand what was happening. I said to my mother as the train pulled out, 'my daddy is going away and never coming back.'

He was gone for three months while he attended basic training at Wagga Wagga Airforce Base. He was then posted to the RAAF base at Williamtown NSW as a Radio Technician. He had very little schooling and prior to joining the RAAF he attended night school for a few years to gain enough qualifications to apply for that position. When we moved to Williamtown my parents rented a flat in Stockton just north of Newcastle. While there, I attended year 1 at Stockton Primary School.

My love for airplanes grew from a very young age. It was a standing joke with my family and friends, that whenever my mother asked me if I would like to go to the beach, I said no because I wanted to go to the airport and see the planes. So off we would go to the airport where I dreamed of being in control of the 707 or Fokker Friendship and flying it through the skies to all the exotic places in the world.

In 1966 my father was posted to Amberley Air Force base, so we moved back to Brisbane where I attended Wilston State School before moving onto Newmarket High School. I excelled in long distance running and was school champion in the annual long-distance race in year nine and ten. I represented in the Queensland schoolboys' championships at Lang Park as it was known in those days before being renamed Suncorp Stadium.

While attending year nine I met my first love, Debra. She was a beautiful young woman and very shy. She lived in a house on a very high hill overlooking the suburb of Alderley. I walked her home every day and finally worked up the courage one day to ask her for a kiss. She replied by kissing me. I felt like I was walking on air all the way home.

Her father was a true Australian who never missed a day's work no matter how sick he was. Her mother was a strict church goer, and unfortunately, I was not the 'chosen one' for her daughter. We never got on from the start. After I left school, I used to meet Debra around the corner as she was two and a half years younger than me and wasn't allowed out at that stage. When she completed year 10, she left school and attended technical college to complete an administration course and then gained employment with the Brisbane City Council.

I never liked school and still had the urge for adventure in me. I finally convinced my parents that school was not my forte. Just before my fifteenth birthday, my mother said that if I could find an apprenticeship, I could leave school. The next day I collected my pushbike and rode around to the panel beating shops. The owner of the second shop I approached said, 'we are looking for a new apprentice, but I need to talk to your parents first.' I don't remember the ride home. I was that excited because I had found the job I wanted.

So, with my parents' permission, I started working at the Enoggera Motor Body Works as an apprentice panel beater. My mentor Ross was a knowledgeable man who taught me a lot. I still had time for sport of course and played Rugby League. I spent a season playing for Brothers leagues club 'the leprechauns' in under sixteens. Then I moved to the Northern Suburb Club 'the devils' at Nundah.

Debra and I were still together. She would come on the team bus with me and watch my games. She had grown into a lovely lady and was a confident woman who had overcome her shyness. It was still frowned upon for her to go out with me and definitely not at night. As the restraints were applied by her mother, it was difficult for us to see each other on a regular basis.

I was the kicker for my team, so I always stayed back after training to practice my kicks. During one of these training sessions, I heard a voice behind me say 'I have been watching you and you have what it takes.' It was the famous John Sattler - Gentleman John as he was known to his fans and one of the greatest Rugby League players of all times. He said, 'I would like to give you this brand-new set of Adidas football boots as a gift.' It was a great surprise to me and a true honour.

Next, I joined the Rebel Car and Custom Club at Newstead, along with my good mate from school, Greg. As the youngest members of the club, we were looked after by everyone. We attended the Drag Racing at Surfers Paradise and custom shows at the exhibition grounds in Brisbane. We were allowed to attend the National championships by our parents in both Sydney and Adelaide before I was eighteen. They were special times and the bus trip to Adelaide with all the men and ladies was a great one. We were allowed a beer now and then, but we were looked after by everyone on that trip.

During those years as a club member, I was taught how to drive various Drag cars and given the chance to take a few cars for a test, which I never refused. It was something special: the excitement, the speed, the noise.   One club member gave me a run in his Dragster and as I eased my foot down, I was in seventh heaven.

I didn't stop there of course. Years later, in the front seat of a "RAAF" Royal Australian Air Force Mirage jet, I broke the speed of sound in a flight over the Straits of Malacca off Malaysia. Many years later , I got to fly with the USAF Thunderbirds in an F16 out of Nellis Air Force base Las Vegas. As a qualified pilot then, with over six thousand hours, I was allowed to fly the aircraft "under instruction" and break the sound barrier over the Nevada Desert. And of course, it was a thrill for me!

Brisbane 1973

Chapter 2

Air Force Fire Fighter

The 1970's - a decade that shaped modern Australia - conscription was scrapped, tertiary education was free, the White Australia policy was abolished, and the Vietnam war ended. Attitudes to women and Aboriginals were changing. Star Wars toys came out and the floppy disk and microprocessors were introduced.

The 1970s was a decade that shaped me too. I had left school in 1972 to work as an apprentice panel beater but by 1975, I was looking for more of a challenge in life and joined the Royal Australian Air Force as a firefighter. I did my rookies at Edinburgh Air Force base just outside Adelaide in South Australia. It was the middle of winter and as a Queenslander, I was freezing. I met some wonderful guys during my time in the RAAF who I still keep in contact with today.

After completing my basic course, my trade course as a firefighter wasn't due until the following year, so we had a choice to be based at any RAAF fire section in Australia. I chose Amberley, as my love for flying was growing each day. They had just acquired the F-111 McDonald Douglas aircraft from America, and I wanted to see these aircraft up close. My time at Amberley Air Force base was one of the best times in my military career.

I first visited the recently formed 12th Squadron at the northern end of the base. This squadron was tasked to operate the new Chinook helicopters. I was shown around by the Warrant Officer and introduced to a few pilots. After that day I decided to become an air force pilot. Later I was shown over the 9 Squadron Helicopters "Huey's" as they were known. I was approached by a Squadron Leader who I noticed was a returned Vietnam Veteran by the ribbons on his uniform.

He said, 'I hear you want to become an air force pilot' and I answered yes sir. He asked what education I had, and I admitted, 'not enough to become a pilot as yet sir.' He asked if I was willing to learn and when I said I was, he arranged a meeting for me to visit the Squadron Leader at the Education Section.

The next day, I reported to the Education Section. The Squadron Leader asked me why I wanted to become a RAAF pilot and what education I had. I told him that I had left school before completing year ten, but he said that was not an issue if I wanted to learn. I started my course one week later and completed my year twelve senior equivalent a few years later. I was so proud to have achieved such a personal step in my life. My dream was nearly complete. Wing Commander Stephens arranged for me to go in front of a RAAF selection panel. This process was just completed before I was posted to RAAF Base Butterworth in Malaysia. I was advised to take the posting even though I was concerned it might affect my chances of gaining a position on one of the next few pilot courses.

During my time at Amberley, in 1976, a major exercise took place called "Kangaroo 2". This involved several overseas countries. During this exercise I was offered a flight on the USAF 707 refuelling tanker. Arriving early the following morning, I noticed the United States Air Force "USAF KC-135" on the hard stand across from where I reported for the debriefing. This aircraft is a modified Boeing 707. It was converted into a tanker to refuel aircraft in flight.

On the morning of the flight, I reported to equipment section to be kitted out in my flying gear and was also fitted with a parachute, 'number 13'. I never thought that this was an unlucky number. Soon afterwards I was collected by the American aircrew and driven to the aircraft. The mission was to fly to a position east of Mackay in Queensland to refuel several F-14 Tomcats. Then stay on station for a few more hours to refuel other aircraft before returning to Amberley.

After departing on time, we headed towards our first reporting position, Heron Island. I had the best seat in the house, what they call the jump seat which is centred behind the captain of the aircraft and the co-pilot. Major Louis the captain was explaining to me their mission today in more detail when he noticed a red light that appeared in the cockpit. Suddenly both pilots became very busy, books were called for and both pilots were searching for check lists. They explained to me the red light indicated a major hydraulic oil leak and this problem could lead to undercarriage failure on our return to Amberley.

The crew were summoned to the flight deck and told to search the aircraft for any sign of major oil leaks. Hatches were unscrewed as the search went on with no sign of any oil leaks. In the meantime, Major Louis made a radio call to his ground crew indicating the problem and it was decided to abort the mission and declare a 'PAN' which stands for Possible Assistance Needed. This is only one step below a Mayday. Major Louis radioed back to flight control that they were declaring a PAN and wanted immediate clearance to return to Amberley. Within 30 seconds we were given direct clearance.

The next problem that arose was the amount of fuel we were carrying. The KC-135 tanker had a maximum transfer fuel load of 200,000 lbs (90,719 kilograms) when fully loaded, and we were. Major Louis contacted his ground crew again asking for clearance to dump fuel just before his return back to Amberley. The answer back was NO.

With that large amount of fuel, the aircraft was well above its prescribed landing weight. This meant a different approach was needed to land the aircraft without causing any major damage. Air traffic instructed Major Louis to fly west of Amberley to an area called the Darling Downs and begin a left hand 5-minute holding pattern.

Then Major Louis made a call that all unnecessary crew were to prepare to bail out over the Darling Downs. I could not believe what I was hearing. I left my seat to collect my parachute and noticed the number 13 written on the front. I thought, 'maybe 13 is unlucky'! As the crew members and I donned our helmets and chutes we tried to make fun of this unbelievable event. Just then the order was reversed.

We found out later that the Australian Air Force didn't want one of their airmen jumping out of a perfectly good aircraft. I saved the day. The crew were so happy about this decision they rewarded me with lots of free beer after we landed back at Amberley that evening.

A few months later I was invited to go for a flight on a RAAF Bell Iroquois UH-1 by Flight Lieutenant Stephens, whose call sign was 'Ghost. He was a respected Vietnam veteran who had flown many missions during the war. We got on very well and became long time friends.

As we were preparing to take off FLTLT Stephens said they were tasked to fly up to the northern tip of Frazer Island and check on fires that had been burning for some time on the island. Stephens was known for many antics during his career as a helicopter pilot. It was mentioned that this could have affected his promotions, and I was about to see why.

As we arrived on task, we flew around with both doors locked back and reported back to base. Shortly after, FLTLT Stephens said over the radio that he had arranged to meet a trawler out at sea. So, we headed in an easterly direction. After fifteen minutes we came across a large trawler and descended to about 100 feet above the deck. I was wondering what was going on when FLTLT Stephens said, 'do you want some prawns for lunch?' I said that would be great.

A crewman lowered the rescue cable down to the trawler crew, who attached a large bag. We pulled it up and then departed back to Frazer Island where we feasted on freshly cooked king prawns with loaves of fresh bread, lemons and tartar sauce. How good was that? I was told what happens here stays here, and a word was never mentioned on my return.

After we had finished, we cleaned up and as we were getting airborne FLTLT Stephens mentioned dessert. After the prawn stunt, I wondered what he was talking about.

As we approached the town of Nambour we started to descend. FLTLT Stephens pointed to the "Big Pineapple" and said we are pulling in as they have the best desserts.

Then "Ghost" proceeded to land the helicopter alongside the car park. As we removed our flight gear a van pulled up to take us to the main entrance where we were greeted by the manager. It was a fabulous place, and the cakes and pies were delicious!

After about an hour we were driven back to the helicopter and departed, much to the amazement of the crowd of people gathered below. As we approached Ipswich FLTLT Stephens told me he would show me where he lived and introduce me to his wife. As we approached the suburb of Bundamba, he descended the helicopter to about 800 ft and circled his house until his wife came out.

Now I knew why we got on so well. We were both rebels.

One of the funniest incidents that happened to me was during the massive Kangaroo 2 exercise involving the Americans and Kiwis, and of course the Australians.

We were housed on base with the Americans, and we got on very well with them. We had large gum trees outside of our accommodation blocks which were home to a number of koalas. The Americans were intrigued by these animals and wanted to take them home.

A few days before Kangaroo 2 was completed, the parties started. There was a lot of drinking, eating pizza and we told them that we would be auctioning off the koalas for the Americans to take home. Yes, it was true, they actually thought they could take them home.

So, the auction went ahead, much to the bemusement of the Australian military personnel present. The head auctioneer 'name withheld' was from armament section and had previous experience as an auctioneer in the outback of Australia. No one could believe this was actually going to go ahead. The first four koalas were sold for $250 USD. Then one of the new purchasers asked how do they collect them? The answer was quite simple. 'You have to climb the tree to get them' the auctioneer replied.

Next thing the place erupted with military police entering the large room from every door. USAF and RAAF military police filled the room quickly. I was sitting in a lounge chair at the time of the bust and immediately closed my eyes slumped in the chair pretending I was asleep. The military Police arrested everyone who was awake and strangely left those who were unconscious or asleep. Later I found out the reason for the raid was some small dummy bombs were taken from one of the hangers and found in a room a few doors down. Needless to say, the koalas remained in their trees and the Americans got their money back!

In 1982, my seventh year in the Air Force, I got married for the first time, had a son, and was posted to RAAF base Butterworth in Malaysia.

While I was in Butterworth Sir James Killen AC, KCMG arrived for a visit. I had previously written letters to Sir James, who was Defence Minister at the time. I really admired this man and his never give up attitude. Every time I would receive a handwritten letter back, which amazed me that a person in such a position had the time to communicate with someone like me.

I was on duty at Crash Section one morning when the watchkeeper received a phone call asking for LAC Hughes to report to Air Commodore Reynold's office. I was replaced and proceeded to the OC's office on the section pushbike. I was nervous because the base commander wanted to see me personally. This is not the way the chain of command works.

Suddenly, out walks the Air Commodore with Sir James Killen. You could have blown me over with a feather. I still didn't know what was going on. Then Air Commodore Reynolds said to me 'LAC please follow us into my room'. When the door closed. I was nearly wetting myself. Then Sir James shook my hand and told me to sit down.

Air Commodore Reynolds said, 'I'm sure you are wondering why you are here. Sir James told me that the two of you have been communicating over the past years and now he needs somebody he can trust to show him around Butterworth and Penang before he goes back to Canberra. Most importantly,' the Air Commodore continued, 'Sir James' visit is not to be mentioned to anyone.'

Outside the rear entrance was a non-military sedan car with Sir James' private driver who drove me back to the barracks. I had been told to change into civilian clothes. I was shaking so much I couldn't get my foot into my pants. I was simply stunned. After we returned in record time, Sir James entered the back of the car with me and shook hands again.

He said 'Son, show me the highlights. I need a stiff scotch now.' I told him there was a bar just outside the base and he said, 'what are we waiting for, son?' That name stuck with me whenever we met up until he passed away in 2007.

As the car pulled up outside the bar, we alighted and I asked, 'What kind of scotch would you like, Sir James?' He said, 'no, what would you like to drink?' I told him that I was still on duty so I would have a lime juice. I remember him laughing and saying to me 'I am your boss!' I thought, *yes you do outrank me just a tad*. He asked again, 'ok son what would you like? I am paying for today's little tour'. I got the message and said, 'I will have an Anchor beer, Sir James.'

Next Sir James asked me where there was a good place to eat. I took him to the Restaurant Wah Kok. It has the best Crispy Rice Soup dish around and the chicken is amazing. We had a feast with a few more scotches and beers. Later, we boarded the ferry to Penang Island. On our arrival we did some shopping and parked outside the well-known Tiger bar.

All in all, I had a great time with Sir James. It was one of many highlights during my time in the Air Force, and I was able to build a friendship with him in the years after. I attended his 80th birthday party and met numerous luminaries of the Whitlam Era, including Gough himself, and his wife Margaret. Sir James was a remarkable man who contributed greatly to modern Australia.

Being a firefighter in the air force was exciting work but I also had a lot of fun and witnessed some pretty exciting events as well.

I was told two great stories that I will pass on now. Around the mid-seventies at the Williamstown RAAF Base, just north of Newcastle, a pilot was doing his conversion course onto a Mirage jet at the start of his operational career. All Mirages at the time were equipped with dual seater models for training purposes as well as ejection seats.

As the Mirage was turning on final approach, an unsafe left wheel indicator light flashed and on landing the left wheel collapsed on the roll out. As the pilots later explained, 'we left the runway on the left-wing tip and in full afterburner.'

Two RAAF firefighters saw the incident unfold, mounted their truck and sped towards the runway just before the crash alarm bells sounded for a full turnout of all fire trucks.

As the two firefighters drove towards the Mirage, the pilot pushed the throttles forward into afterburner, causing the aircraft to gather speed, nose high, rapidly heading straight toward the fire truck. Next thing the fire truck made a massive swerve as the Mirage passed just behind them, clipping the meteorological hut and becoming airborne again after hitting the raised section of the high-speed taxiway.

The Mirage passed about 100 meters from the tower and 10 meters behind the fire truck, showering rocks and debris all over it. The Mirage looked like it was going to collide with one of the large hangers but managed to get above them as the conversion pilot ejected over the base. The second ejection was above the base perimeter (main gate).

The pilots' lives were saved that day by good luck and good management. Without the efforts of all concerned, it could have ended in a smoking mess.

So bloody close! Bill, one of the firefighters said he still remembers the Mirage heading toward the flight line with personnel running in all directions. Another pilot told Bill later, that he had just been strapped into a jet when the ground crew suddenly abandoned him. He looked up and knew why.

When everyone gathered later for a debrief, Bill and the other firefighter informed the Senior Air Traffic Controller (SATCO) and the Commanding Officer (CO) that the Mirage was so close, they could see the pilots' names on their helmets. They both scoffed at that. When Bill described their insignias and mentioned that a Bruce Wood was in the back seat, the SATCO asked, 'how would you bloody know that?' Bill replied, 'his name was on the helmet.'

The CO shook his head and exclaimed, 'it was bloody close then!' Indeed, it was sir, indeed it was.

The pilot doing the conversion went on to have a long and successful career, retiring as Air Marshal, 'Chief of the Airforce' in 2008.

There were some funny stories as well.

One balmy Sunday afternoon in late 1969 (before my time in the RAAF), two men, Bill and Dave, were on the afternoon domestic crew. They noted that the CDW (Commonwealth Department of Works) had left their ride on mower just around the corner of the hangar and could not resist the temptation. They promptly started it, racing around the tarmac and through the hangar.

During one of the ventures through the hanger, Bill skidded behind one of the fire trucks collecting the silver coated rescue suit. Unfortunately, the leg and the shoulder of the said suit received severe lacerations. The next morning when the suit was discovered, the Flight Sergeant was furious. Accompanied by the Flight Lieutenant, he found Bill and Dave and demanded to know, 'what the hell happened?'

Just then, two large black dogs ran past from behind the hangar. In perfect harmony, Bill and Dave called out, 'that's them! That's the dogs we seen dragging the suit around the hanger and we chased them off.'

One of the Airfield Defence Guards said the dogs belonged to the Commanding Officer. The Flight Sergeant said that the CO should be formally notified of this, and he was not happy. As Bill and Dave walked back to the fire section, they passed the Flight Lieutenant, who retorted out of earshot of others, 'dogs my arse!' No more said. What a guy!

***

Question: Who was the airman who was completing his basic fire course at Point Cook in Victoria in the early

21

seventies when he was carrying out a drill on the TFR "Truck Fire Rescue" with a Sgt Allan sitting beside him. The airman in question engaged the wrong lever and filled the inside of the fire truck with foam!

***

One day at RAAF Fire Section Laverton, a certain LAC (leading aircraftsman) was responsible for disfiguring a Warrant Officers shirt.

The Warrant Office never really understood his troops and thought of himself as a God. The respect he thought he warranted was never there. He was one to always wave his finger in front of the person he was giving instructions to, and this was thought of as belittling.

So, one day before parade, this LAC entered the Warrant Officer locker before he arrived for parade and drew a big Z for Zorro on the back of his parade uniform.

Well, when he finally caught on, it caused a massive disruption amongst the troops. The troops were running everywhere, trying to hide except the LAC who when confronted by the warrant officer and said, 'me sir? I would never think of doing anything like that.' A protected species one must think. For those who were around, do the initials J.M. ring a bell?

***

Being shift workers, we firefighters always had a good relationship with the cooks at the mess hall. When we were rostered for night shift, we had rations allocated for our evening meal but when we went to the mess to pick them up, we would talk the cook on duty into giving us a bit extra. We put that into the refrigerator for the day shift to cook up.

Unfortunately, there was one firefighter who was so mean and stingy that he pilfered any extra rations. We were sick of this, so one night when the cook gave us some massive beef sausages, we decided to take action. On the way back to fire section we called into medical and collected a syringe from the Orderly.

The foam we used in the 1970's to put out fires was basically a blood and bone mixture which smelt like rotten garden fertiliser. The big beef sausages were duly pumped full of the foam using the syringe. They were placed in the refrigerator and the trap was set for the tea leaf to knock them off and take them home to supplement his food bill.

Wrong. He apparently didn't like beef sausages, so he left them. And when the new shift reported for duty no one checked to make sure the bait was taken.

Just before morning break, one of the airmen on the day shift put the large sausages into a frying pan and placed the pan on the stove to simmer. As the sausages swelled, they burst the skin, and a horrible mess of foul-smelling foam and sausage meat poured all over the stove top and on to the floor. The blame went straight back to the cooks. 'Bloody cooks have set us up again!' We never had the gumption to own up to that one!

***

Later, we were given new fire extinguishers that had two chemicals in them which reacted together to produce foam, an A and B charge. One was placed into the inner container with a lead stopper on it. The other was mixed with water and placed into the fire extinguisher. When turned over, the inner container escaped and mixed with the other chemical and foam was produced and poured out of the nozzle under pressure.

Every Monday was panic night for the single airmen that lived on base. They had to ensure their rooms, and the ablution blocks were spotless for inspection. So, for a prank we waited until after midnight on inspection day, went into a double storey block and placed a double charge in each of the toilet cisterns and two of the other charges into the toilet bowls.

Apparently, it was mayhem the next morning as everyone was rushing to the toilets before they were off limits for inspection. Of course, as soon as the flush button was pushed, the chemical reacted and being much lighter than water, the foam poured out of the bowls and all over the floors of the toilet block.

They knew they had been gotten by the firefighters but not who the actual culprits were. We never owned up to that one either.

***

In Butterworth, the Royal Australian Air Force was stationed with the Royal Malaysian Air Force. Contingents of RAAF firefighters and their families would usually be on a 3-year tour before being posted back to Australia.

During 1984 a certain LAC (yes, it was me) was told by a much-disliked Warrant Officer that he was not allowed to leave the fire section due to disciplinary matters. This Warrant Officer was never respected by many of his firefighters due to his incompetence and stupidity.

However, I received a phone call from the Commanding Officer of 3 Squadron who said I had to present myself to the squadron immediately as a flight in a mirage jet was planned in one hour. As I was due to be posted back to Australia and as I played volleyball with the Jet-Jocks (a volleyball team which consisted of the Malaysian pilots) the flight had been arranged as a parting gift. Well, this could cause a dilemma since I was confined to the section.

Being able to pull a rabbit out of a hat I thought of a plan that could work because the Warrant Officer was out of the section for some time on business. I approached my newly promoted Sergeant who I had worked with on other bases in Australia and told him my dilemma. The Sergeant was known for his discretion and someone who you would trust with your life. Being in charge of the LAC and under instructions from the Warrant Officer that the LAC was not to leave the section he stood by me and placed himself in the line of fire should I not be found at the section on the return of the Warrant Officer. The Sergeant told me to go but try not to be too long.

I reported to 3 squadron and was taken through an in depth debrief of what I should do in an emergency if I needed to eject in flight. The dual seater had one canopy, and the pilots sat behind each other. I was told if an emergency happened and the words 'eject, eject, eject' were said and I didn't pull the ejection seat release, I could be seriously injured by the rockets of the front seat leaving the aircraft.

I prepared for my flight and was introduced to my pilot. I was fitted with a G-suit and a helmet with an oxygen mask. The pilot and I then proceeded to the aircraft.

After the aircraft was checked over by the pilot, we took turns climbing the ladder to enter the cockpit. We were strapped into the seats and our oxygen masks connected and checked. Next the pilot checked communications with the front seat then ignited the jet engine and received a taxi clearance to hold at the southern threshold. As the aircraft started to taxi, the pilot lowered the canopy. The best was yet to come.

As the Mirage taxied towards the southern end of the field it had to pass by the fire section. I knew the firemen were playing volleyball outside and I wanted to wave to them.

As the Mirage came by the fire section all they could see from the front of Mirage was the LAC waving furiously. Next thing I saw was a white Land Rover pull up outside of the section. This meant one thing, both the Sergeant and I were going to be in the shit big time after I arrived back at the section.

The Mirage received a clearance to taxi onto the runway and then received a further take-off clearance to Flight Level 400. The pilot advanced the controls to After burner stage. As the aircraft started rolling, I noticed in the distance the Warrant Officer waving his arms in front of the Sergeant and then the aircraft was airborne heading into space.

On returning after a 60 min flight, I was presented with a Mach Busters certificate to commemorate breaking the speed of sound. I proceeded back to the fire section where I was told to report to the Warrant Officer. When I reported to the office the Sergeant was already there. The door was closed, and many words were spoken - some that cannot be repeated. Then after a few minutes the door opened, and both the LAC and Sergeant excited the office with smiles ear to ear. The Warrant Officer excited his office, entered his land rover, and disappeared in a ball of smoke, not at all happy. Nothing was ever mentioned again by the Warrant Officer but to this day the Sergeant and the LAC are much talked about. I really enjoyed that flight and it is one I will never forget.

***

In all, I served a standard tour of duty of nine years with the RAAF. This was my higher education path. I completed high school and further courses that I needed to fulfil my dream to become a pilot. During those nine years I also got to serve my country and be a part of something greater than myself.

As a RAAF firefighter, I saw very few fires. We were there primarily to make sure they didn't happen, and we were good at the job. By the end of my tour, I was ready to go out in the civilian world and put those skills to work. Some of the hardest things I would ever do in my life where yet to come. The military had provided me with a top-class education and a bag full of tools. It was time for me to give that back to my country as a civilian firefighter.

Chapter 3

Brisbane Fire Fighter

By the 1980s, as I finished my time in the military, the Australian economy was booming, Property values skyrocketed, and many businesses made large profits. Many people became pre-occupied with making money and of course, spending it. Fashion, music and television from the decade was glitzy, showy and glamorous. The 1980s is sometimes called the 'me decade'. Home computers were taking off and notable inventions included the CD-ROM, Apple MacIntosh and Windows. In 1987 stock markets crashed and Australia suffered a recession. Many environmental causes came to the forefront of public debate. By the 1980s, migrants from all over the world had settled in Australia and multiculturalism was embraced. In 1988 Australia celebrated its bicentennial.

In 1982 I was in the RAAF and posted to Malaysia. On my return to Australia, I decided to leave the armed forces and continue my flying studies in civilian life. With my previous firefighting experience, I gained a position with the Fire Service in Brisbane which allowed me plenty of time to study and advance my pilot skills in civilian life.

When I completed my initial training at Enoggera Fire Station in Brisbane. I was transferred to Head Quarters Kemp Place near the Story Bridge in Brisbane City. Still wet behind the ears, I was hoping for a fire so I could prove myself to the senior firefighters that I was capable and trustworthy.

Days, then weeks went by, and I thought: *every other shift has had two or more fires of one sort or another and here I am with no fires.* As Kemp Place is the headquarters, the strength of the crews on each shift are over by at least one or two personnel, to replace any firefighters that report in sick or are injured on shift at other fire stations. This certain nightshift my name was called over the PA system to report to the duty room. I was told to gather my turnout gear and report to Annerley Fire Station for the completion of my night shift.

It was the first time I went to another station, and I was excited. Annerley is a two-pump station because the Princess Alexandria Hospital is nearby. As I pulled up, I was met by Max, the Station Officer. He introduced himself and seemed a really nice guy. I was taken in and introduced to the other guys and told I was number two on first pump.

I placed my turnout gear on the back seat and checked the vehicle over as normal. Being a junior firefighter, it doesn't matter what station you go to, you are the centre of all the jokes, but you expect that and take it in your stride. You have to earn your stripes and prove you are a capable firefighter who can be trusted.

I was also introduced to a senior firefighter called Boots who was tasked to look after me that night. He was number 1 on the fire truck I was assigned, a 30-year veteran who I looked up to as I had heard so much about this guy. He attended the famous Whiskey a Go-Go fire. He told me that it was the worst fire he had ever attended and was stuck in his mind forever. Little did I know back then that I would experience the same mental torture.

At about 8 pm the lights flashed, and bells rang. The voice over the PA system said: 'turnout to a shop on fire on Logan Road at Greenslopes,' a suburb 5 kilometres away. My emotions erupted and I felt both scared and happy. My time had arrived where I could prove myself.

The two vehicles left the Annerley Fire Station with sirens sounding out loud and red lights flashing in the night sky as we headed up Logan Road. I donned my breathing apparatus while Boots told me that when we arrived, I was to collect the standpipe from the rear of the truck and find the hydrant. He said there was one on the intersection of Logan and Chatsworth Roads across from the Greenslopes Bowling Alley as he handed me the hydrant book to double check. As we arrived, I saw about five shops in a row and the last shop was well alight.

Immediately, I jumped out of the truck, collected the brass standpipe and ran up to the intersection looking for the hydrant cover. I imagined how this area 30 mins before would have been so quiet and then all of a sudden it turned into a fire ground with smoke covering the area, flashing lights of red and blue, the voices of firefighters trying to be heard over the noise of the fire and me trying to find water for the pump. I was in the area shown to me on the hydrant book, but I couldn't find the hydrant cover on that roadway.

The pump operator was yelling out for water as they were using the smaller lines and could not change over to the bigger hose until they were connected to a water supply. As my blood pressure rose, I thought *keep your cool Kevin, you will find it.* Then, I remembered another hydrant on the chart up Chatsworth Road, about 50 meters away. Straight away I found the hydrant, yelled out 'plug!', lifted the cover, connected the standpipe, and cracked the water. This is to clean any dirty water from the pipes before it enters the fire pump. Mal from the other fire truck connected the big line and turned on the hydrant.

I ran back towards the fire to report to Boots. I quickly donned my BA mask and checked I had a good seal. My BA tag was removed, and I was connected to a lanyard. I was handed a charged hose and told to meet Boots inside. As I entered the shop my heart was pumping - it felt like someone was banging on my chest. I instantly lost any visual reference, and it was so hot I thought I was going to fry. I could just see the small hose and could hear Boots yelling out. I yelled back, because we had BA sets on and our masks muffled the sounds when we spoke. I found Boots and handed him the charged large hose. He handed me the smaller hose and said, 'concentrate your line toward those flames in front of you'.

As I opened the hose, I had this sudden adrenalin rush. I felt finally I had been blooded and I was putting into practice what I had been taught as a rookie firefighter. After about 25 mins we had the fire well beaten and we handed our lines over to the other crew and moved back outside. The shop was a Speed Shop and dealt in motor parts. It was established an electrical fault started the fire.

This was my first introduction to news crews as they approached both Boots and me. The lights from the TV cameras flashed in our eyes and next thing I hear Boots yell out some certain words after which they all departed looking elsewhere for their story. As we were packing up our Station Officer came over to us both and said a job well done and 'Boots, you got to stop treating the news crews like that. They are only doing their job.' Boots had his reasons as he explained to me later - it involved a bad incident at the Whiskey a Go-Go fire.

After we arrived back at the station and cleaned all the gear, I reported to the Station Officer who shook my hand and said I did a great job, and I will make a good firefighter. I said to Max 'I couldn't find the Hydrant.' He said he heard I had problems then said, 'don't worry, neither could I, it was covered by the new bitumen they just laid. It was good thinking on your part to move onto another one and to know where it was.' So, I felt a lot better that I did my job the best I could.

As it was approaching 11 pm, Max told us to go to bed. So as usual I checked my bed before climbing in and sure enough a plastic snake was in my bed which I felt and removed. No one owned up to the joke, but I never let on either. I am sure they were waiting for me to yell out.

At four in the morning, on came the lights and with bells ringing I quickly bounced out of bed to a voice over the PA saying, 'turn out to a fire with Roma Street Fire Station at Melbourne Street South Brisbane - multiple calls. As I was running to the fire truck and still coming out of a deep sleep I thought, 'two in one night'. Only truck 1 was required to roll in support of the Roma Street crew. After the station officer spoke on the radio to the communications room, he turned to me and said, 'you are certainly learning your trade tonight.'

As we arrived together with Roma Street crew, Max told me to go with Boots on case 1. We checked our BA masks; our tags were taken, and we proceeded to a side door which I opened with a master key. It became one of my most loved pieces of equipment! a large sledgehammer.

The building was a double story brick building built around the 1930's with interior timber floors. The fire was confined to the ground level and our main aim was to stop the spread to the upper level.

Other crews entered through the front door, and we soon were getting on top of this fire when someone close to us yelled out 'gas!' Immediately I thought, *we are gone*. It was a word no firefighter wants to hear in the middle of a fire. By some marvellous intervention from above, the gas was isolated before anything major happened. Being a fish and chip shop, it was established the fire started from one of the cooking tubs that was left on. The gas leak was caused by a collapsing timber beam which struck a pipe and caused a leak. The gas inspector said he has no idea how it never exploded maybe killing everyone in the building. This was the first time I escaped death but not the last.

During my six years in the Brisbane Fire Brigade and during the change over to the Queensland Fire Service I attended more than thirty emergences and numerous false alarms. These included eighteen structural fires, eight road accidents, two confined space rescues, one ship fire, and two flood rescues.

The mateship was something I will never forget. It was a very special bond between firefighters as proven worldwide especially after the 9/11 tragedy. The trust you have in each other is second to none especially where you can face potential death at any time.

In total sixty firefighters from Queensland have died fighting fires since 1877. I lost a very close friend in 1989:

Firefighter Christopher John Warburton at a house fire in Highgate Hill on Brisbane southside. R.I.P Chris.

No matter who was cooking the evening meal they all got given a serve by all the other firefighters on how it was going to turn out and whether it was palatable. Just a bit of banter between each other was a sign how well we bonded and got on together. When junior firefighters were assigned a station after finishing their basic course, it took months before trust was established. That is the way it is and always will be.

Every bit of equipment on a fire vehicle is placed in a particular position so you know where it is at all times. As a junior firefighter I remember spending hours going through the various vehicles learning where each piece of equipment is and learning how to use it.

You always checked your personal equipment before placing it on the fire vehicle as you never knew who's turn it was to be the centre of a joke. Things they use to do was cover the head strap of your helmet with black boot polish or Vaseline, put honey in your turnout coat pockets or fill your boots with water. They were great days.

Each turnout, every firefighter has a role to play on route to an alarm. Back in the early 80's on Pump one the number one firefighter would take a card from a box inside of the vehicle matching the particular building in alarm. He would read the directions from this card to the driver. Turn left out of station then first right etc. If the alarm was to a house fire in a certain street a street directory would be looked up so as to give the driver directions. Now it is all fed automatically on a printout from the station attending the fire, along with GPS coordinates.

The number two firefighter took the hydrant book and looked up the street in which the alarm or fire is and find the nearest hydrant. On arrival he would grab the standpipe, find the hydrant and connect it. He made a quick run back to the truck to collect the hose end from the pump operator then ran back to the standpipe, connect the hose and turn the water on. This gave a constant supply of water to the fire vehicle pump.

On returning to the station a firefighter from each vehicle must alight to help guide the vehicle back into the allotted bay. The driver then alights and plugs the 240-volt battery charging cable back into the vehicle to make sure it is always ready to start. As the ladder crew remained back, they were tasked with cleaning up the dishes from dinner. Everyone knew their job and we were all proud to be part of B Crew.

Depending on the night's activities we always had lectures if they could be arranged due to turnouts and other duties.

An area we specialised in were ship fires. These are some of the most dangerous fires any firefighter could ever be involved in. At Roma Street Fire Station, we have a special crew that look after all the breathing apparatus repairs and training. Re-training is carried out on a regular basis as there is no room for mistake in a real fire situation. Part of the Roma Street Fire Station is made up of a ships internal hull where every Brisbane firefighter must pass a bi-annual test. The ship's hull is filled full of smoke and heat and dummies are placed throughout the hull and structures.

You are paired off with another firefighter and told how many dummies are in there that need rescuing. You put on your breathing apparatus; each firefighter checks the other's bottle and mask then you tie off a length of rescue line and tie off each other with a lanyard. You then descend down into the hull where the temperatures are very high, and the visibility is zero. Everything you touch is hot, and you have 35 minutes to rescue the allotted dummies. It is hot exhausting work however working in pairs, if it is done right, will result in achieving your goal.

Before we retire for the night, we left our turnout coat on the seat of the vehicle we were assigned to and placed our boots beside our bed with our pants over the boots and our braces open, all ready to jump into quickly.

It is very important that you are up, dressed and in the fire vehicle before it leaves the station. I have been witness to a few firefighters who miss their vehicle because they were too slow getting out of bed. They certainly received a severe reprimand from the Officer in Charge. Today I would think you might be lucky to keep your job.

We never had all the modern equipment like they have today, but we got by.

After being promoted to first class firefighter I assumed the role as number one on the first pump. A junior firefighter is usually number two on first pump and his role is to keep an eye on any potential danger that could happen. If he saw anything dangerous, he would tap number one on the shoulder or pull him back. The trust you have in each other is enormous. It is a team effort that is very special.

Chapter 4

On The Rescue Truck

Some of the toughest incidents I ever faced was when I became a driver on the rescue truck. Around the mid-eighties there were three rescue trucks in the Brisbane Fire Service. One in Kemp Place Headquarters, one in Roma Street Station and one at Mount Gravatt station. Each truck had multiple rescue tools including the jaws of life, hydraulic air bags, oxy acetylene sets, hydraulic rams, ropes and much, much more. It took weeks of training to gain a position on this special fire truck.

The truck was manned by a Sub Station Officer and a firefighter/driver. You not only had to know how to use each piece of equipment you had to know what the physical capabilities of each piece were, what they could withstand and all their internal workings. Each piece of specialist equipment had its place and if asked at any time you had to produce the piece straight away then explain it workings and how you might use it. The day I was promoted to the rescue truck was a special time in my life. It meant I was now classed as a highly trained senior firefighter.

I clearly remember my first road accident, it was a multi vehicle accident on the western freeway in Brisbane's west where 4 vehicles were involved, and two vehicles had trapped persons. We set off from Roma Street under siren with lights flashing. My substation officer Terry was a great mentor.

As we rolled, we had multiple radio calls from the Communications centre informing us that Taringa and Moggill Fire trucks were also rolling to the incident. Then we had a further call informing us that police reported six trapped persons in two cars, and two of these were children. As we proceeded down Milton Road and through Toowong, we came to the large roundabout near the Toowong cemetery. As I slowed coming to the roundabout a car went up the inside of me and he sideswiped me nearly causing us to roll. I stopped at the roundabout, but the driver just kept going.

Terry got out of the vehicle to check the damage, but it looked okay, so off we went again. Four km down the road there was a large back up of traffic. The only way around the traffic jam was to jump the centre strip and drive up the oncoming side. As we arrived at the scene of the accident, it looked like a war zone. Bits of metal everywhere. I was guided to a spot near one of the vehicles. The Station Officer had already accessed the scene and previously radioed us informing us of his intentions on our arrival. He met us and said it looked like there were a couple of deceased persons including a child in the red car.

As the two ambulances arrived Terry came back over to me and said, 'it looks bad Kev, we will start with the jaws on the red car.' I got a few other firefighters to help me get the jaws of life out and a few other pieces of equipment and place them nearby. While I fitted my safety gear the screaming from the trapped people was deafening. I felt sick but I ignored it as much as I could and started cutting. We removed the roof, and I then cut through the side pillar to expose the driver and rear passenger's side.

What I saw filled me with despair and horror. Not only were there two adults trapped in the front of the car, but there were also three children trapped in the back seat. One was around two years of age and still in the baby capsule. The two older children were down on the floor behind the front seats. These children were unaccounted for in the initial assessment from the police as they were hidden by all the debris thrown about in the car and the crushed seats.

As the ambulance paramedics moved in for their initial assessment, I heard one say that the female passenger was deceased, but the male driver was still alive and needed to be extracted as soon as possible, as another paramedic inserted a drip into the man's lower arm. I then heard another ambulance crew say that both children behind the front seats were deceased, but the baby was alive. I continued with the Jaws of Life, cutting away part of the front driver's side dash so the man could be removed.

As soon as the man and baby were out of the car, I had to cut away more of the mangled wreck to remove the two deceased children and the deceased woman. As I assisted removing her from the passengers' side of the front seat, I remember the other firefighter saying, 'we will lift on three, one, two, three.' Before I lifted her, I was warned by one of the paramedics that her stomach was perforated, and her intestines were exposed. As we lifted on three, it felt like lifting jelly. Her arms were shattered, and her intestines were sliding out as one of the paramedics applied a white sheet to stop any further loss. I went back to retrieve the Jaws of Life to remove another section of the car so we could reach the two deceased children. This was a job no one would ever want to do.

I have never forgotten those two children and images of them still flash through my mind today. One was a boy aged around five while the girl was a year or two younger. Their bodies looked peaceful but the trauma from the accident had caused horrific injuries. The girl's face was half removed. The boy's arm was partially amputated, and his left leg was twisted back behind his torso. As the other firefighters removed the boy I turned and vomited over the back of the car. It was too much for me to see these beautiful children so horribly mutilated. I was assisted by one of the ambulance officers who said, 'it is never easy seeing deceased children in that state' It was a terrible introduction to my first road accident.

By this time the other crew from Taringa Fire Station had removed the two trapped adults and one child from the other vehicle using crowbars and a porta power hydraulic unit. It is amazing how the damage on one car looks worse, but the occupants escape with minimal injuries.

I walked over to the edge of the highway near the police cars and there was a man being questioned by two police officers. He seemed extremely intoxicated as his speech was unrecognisable. I noticed he was handcuffed, and I heard one of the officers say, 'Your alcohol reading is well over the legal limit, and I am arresting you for further testing.'

The guy was crying and saying that he was sorry. My blood pressure rose through the roof. I have just removed three dead bodies, two of whom are children, and this drunk is saying sorry, as if that matters at this point.

I went over to him coldly and calmly and said, 'see this blood all over me? You caused that and now you have to

43

live with this for the rest of your life. You stole three lives and injured another six innocent souls.' It goes much further than that - families have had their loved ones stolen or injured and first responders' lives are shattered. You never forget.

It was a sombre trip back to the station and not a word was spoken. It was heart wrenching, but everyone handles tragedy in different ways. Some firefighters could not handle the pressures of the job and retired while others just kept turning up shift after shift. Other firefighters still have never seen a good fire or been to a terrible road accident. Maybe they are the lucky ones. Who knows?

When I was stationed at headquarters Kemp Place near the Story Bridge that crosses the Brisbane River. It was not uncommon in the day to have a turnout to people climbing the bridge. Usually, these people's main aim was to commit suicide because of various reasons.

As the police blocked the lanes of traffic heading north and south over the bridge the fire brigade was called to try and rescue the person involved. Being on pump one this night we were called out early one morning with the ladder crew.

After positioning both trucks, the ladder crew got to work setting up the ladder. It was an extension ladder with a bucket on the end where it can hold three to four people. It can be operated from a position at the base of the ladder or from inside the bucket.

I was summoned by the Station Officer from my vehicle and told I would be going up with the Sub Station Officer to rescue the climber. It was my third rescue on the Story Bridge.

Matt the Sub Station Officer and I devised a plan on how we approach the woman and how we would position the ladder with the bucket. We were both connected by a lanyard to a point inside the ladder bucket to prevent us from falling should something happen.

As we approached the woman she started screaming 'Don't come any closer or I will jump!' Matt let me do the talking as he was operating the ladder.

Negotiation is a process where two sides work together to formulate a mutually agreeable outcome for the people involved. Understanding other people's emotions and controlling your own is a critical aspect of negotiations. You need patience and the ability to communicate. Persuasion is directly related to communication and speaking persuasively is a vital aspect of negotiation. Flexibility is also a vital aspect of this process. By being flexible, you may be able to reach a compromise that benefits both parties.

The foundation of negotiation is problem-solving because someone has a problem that requires a solution. Negotiation formats require analytical thinking. Some of the issues you may face during a negotiation may be really complex problems. In these situations, you have to use your initiative, think creatively, be flexible and communicate clearly to find solutions that don't involve suicide. I had completed a course on this just eight months earlier and now my training was put to the test.

We were four meters from the lady, and I said to her, 'let's just be calm and talk slowly.' I introduced myself and Matt and asked for her name. She said Jane. I told her that I was here to help her. 'To help me do that I need to talk to you. Is that okay?' She agreed.

Negotiations went on for an hour before she agreed to let Matt move the ladder closer to her so I could help her into the bucket. Soon we were back on the ground, and everyone was safe.

We were thanked by everyone for our skills and the success of this particular rescue. I was approached by a few senior police officers and introduced to their negotiator who had arrived later on the scene. They heard everything and congratulated me on the way I handled the situation.

Back at the station with the break of dawn approaching I helped Matt complete the necessary paperwork on the incident.

Chapter 5

The Ship Fire

One of the most dangerous incidents I attended was a ship fire. It happened one winter's night when I was based at Kemp Fire Station. We were upstairs in one of the classrooms around 20:00 hrs, when the alarms sounded and the voice over the PA systems said, 'Pumps one and two turn out to a ship fire at the Brisbane Wharf at Lytton'. My first thought was *this is different*. Then I thought: confined space, fire, heat - what kind of cargo is on board? Hopefully it is just a fire, and no one is injured *... or worse*.

As we were heading down Wynnum Road a call came back to send additional ladder crews from both Kemp Place and Roma Street stations. That's when I realised how serious it was. As we approached the ship, we could see people running everywhere like ants around a nest. We were waved through the main gate to a communication point that had been set up. From there we could see thick black smoke pouring from the ship.

As we exited the fire truck our Station Officer went over to the communications point to find out the type of fire on board and what our task was. The radio in the fire truck was full of chatter with one of the other station officers requesting the Breathing apparatus unit from Roma Street and an additional two ambulances. Then my hair stood on end when he requested an isolation area around the wharf of 500 meters to be set up. We all looked at each other. One of the junior firefighters asked, 'how bad is it?' I shook my head, 'bad, by the sound of it'. Fear set in all of us, but we knew this was our job and as a team we would get the job done somehow.

Our officer returned and said to Shane and me, 'get your BAs on. You are tasked to carry out a search and rescue below the rear decks. You've been trained in confined space rescue, so you are the first choice'.

We fitted all our gear and reported to the pump operator from Balmoral who collected our BA tags. We were fitted with rescue ropes and communication radios, then escorted to the boarding ramp. As we boarded the ship, we were met by one of the other station officers who informed us what our precise task would be. It was established a fire had broken out in the engine room and two persons were not accounted for at this time.

We also learned this ship was loading grain and there was a risk of an explosion. There were already a number of firefighters battling the blaze from above. We were shown a map of the layout of the living quarters and work areas so we could get a mental picture of where everything was before we entered. Shane and I worked out a plan and which way we would head first as the unaccounted men were last seen near the communications room.

As I entered below, I looked out in the night sky one more time thinking, *I hope I see you again soon.* Then I gave a thumbs up to the two firefighters looking after our rescue lines.

The visibility was very limited and got worse as we slowly walked deeper into the ship's belly. I made a radio check back to communications and received a 'loud and clear'. We arrived at the entrance to the first room, and everything felt hot to touch. So, I tested the doorknob with the back of my hand. It felt ok, so I opened it, and we checked the first room. I radioed back 'Room 1 all clear'. The reason you feel doorknobs before entering is if the doorknob is too hot and you open the door it can cause what is known as a 'flashback' This can result in serious injury or even death.

After about twenty minutes we had checked a number of living and work areas with no success. The smoke at times seem to dissipate slowly then return to zero visibility. It was extremely hot, humid and exhausting work. Then all of a sudden, a voice come over the radio and said, 'one of the crew has been found and he has informed us that his mate was still on board and last seen in his bed'.

I replied, 'copy that. We will be moving our search to the port side of the ship level C.' This was where the mariner's cabin was situated. With our visibility back down to zero, I knew why the training at Roma Street in the ship's hull was worth it. With the training I had, I knew exactly where I was at any time. You can't afford to become disorientated as it could get you seriously injured or killed.

As we moved to the port side of the ship, we encountered a set of stairs that rose to the level above while another set of stairs opposite that took us down to level C. As we descended, the visibility cleared a little and there below was the mariner laying at the bottom of the stairs, semi-conscious with a badly broken leg and his tibia exposed. Shane immediately radioed back reporting he was found and the state of his condition. I said to Shane, 'I'll have to carry him out as he is.'

I reassured the mariner and told him, 'I have to carry you out over my shoulder. It will hurt.' Shane and I removed our belts and tied them around the mariner's leg, securing them to some extent. I took my mask off to share with the mariner, so he received some fresh air before I refitted my mask and placed him over my right shoulder for the journey back from hell. Shane removed his mask and fed the mariner oxygen as we were ascending the stairs. Shane reported our movements as we climbed each flight. For me, with the dead weight of the injured man on my shoulders, the journey back was exhausting and agonizingly slow.

The two firefighters outside were retrieving the rope as we got closer to the surface. I could hear over the radio a medical crew would be waiting on the wharf for us. As we reached the final two flights of stairs our whistles sounded on our breathing apparatus so loud that could be heard from above. We received a call from the BA crew reminding us we were down to 60 bar pressure, and we needed to return now. Shane confirmed we would be out in a few minutes.

As we started to return to the main deck, I looked up at the final set of stairs and said, 'welcome back'. I carried the mariner over the gang plank and slowly descended to the wharf below before being helped to place the mariner on a waiting stretcher.

Shane and I were met by the Chief Fire Officer who shook our hands and said' that is a rescue you will never forget, and your efforts will be highly commended, congratulations to you both.' We walked over to the BA HAZMAT fire truck which by now had taken over all the operational breathing apparatus. They had boards set up with names and times logged for each breathing apparatus set being used. Their other duty was being the central control point of communications at large fires.

By this time the firefighters were getting the fire under control. If this fire had spread out of control and moved near any of the grain on board, there was potential for a massive explosion. If rapid combustion occurs in a confined space enormous overpressures can build up, causing major structural damage and flying debris. The sudden release of energy from a detonation can produce a shockwave, either in open air or in a confined space. If the spread of flame is at subsonic speed, the phenomenon is sometimes called a 'deflagration', although most of us would call both phenomena 'explosions'

Dust explosions are classified as being either 'primary' or 'secondary' in nature. Primary dust explosions may occur inside process equipment, ships' hulls or similar enclosures, and are generally controlled by pressure relief through purpose build ducting to the external atmosphere. Secondary dust explosions are the result of dust accumulation inside a building being disturbed and ignited by the primary explosion, resulting in a much more dangerous uncontrolled explosion that can affect the entire structure. Historically, fatalities have largely been the result of secondary dust explosions.

These are the necessary conditions required for a dust explosion: - a combustible dust that is dispersed in the air at a sufficiently high concentration; an oxidant (typically atmospheric oxygen); an ignition source (a spark will do), and the area is confined, like a ship. Luckily this night we got on top of the situation and no explosion occurred.

Chapter 6

My Last Night at the Fire Station

Just before completing a shift, we had our hand-over parade and soon after we were dismissed, before heading to our vehicles to drive home or onto our second jobs. This was quite a common practice because many firefighters were also tradesmen. I usually headed down to Eagle Farm to my other employment as an aviation tanker driver.

I was very lucky to secure this position with Shell as there were over 25 applications. I just loved being around aircraft for as long as I could remember. I still wanted to fly jet aircraft and I still dreamed about flying away to exotic destinations. On this day I was refuelling the last Ansett jet to complete my shift before returning to Roma Street fire station for one last night duty.

Arriving at Roma Street, I parked my car out the back then carried my bedding and dinner in. As I reported for duty one of the officers said, 'hey Kev, it's going to be a busy night tonight.'

I said, 'I hope not but it's Friday night.' We all had our superstitions about how busy Friday nights could be. Full moon nights were the same and Friday the 13th was the worst. It was well known in emergency jobs that any shift on these nights was so much busier than other night shifts. More actual fires, road accidents, the incidents increased with no apparent reason.

The shift started with an inspection parade, and we were given our assignments for the night. We were just stowing our gear on the vehicles, when the bells rang out loud and the loudspeaker informed us of a fire at the Brisbane City Town Hall. My position for the shift was number one firefighter on the Pump One truck.

All turn outs in the city involved Pump One and Pump Two. If any alarms involved high rise, hospitals or special buildings the rescue vehicle would deploy as well. The turn table ladder pump would only be dispatched if there was a fire in a building over three stories or special types of fires.

As we arrived at the town hall, I alighted from the truck with my number two man wearing breathing apparatus along with the radio and first aid fire equipment. This is standard practice until it is established there is no fire, or a dangerous situation involved. We quickly realised there was no fire, and I radioed back to the communications room informing them it was a Code 12 – a false alarm. We all returned to our vehicles and returned to the station. I commenced cooking dinner. We always took turns to cook dinner for the crew of 15 firefighters and it was my turn tonight.

No matter who was cooking, they got given a serve by the other firefighters on how it was going to turn out and whether it was edible. The banter was a sign how well we bonded together. When junior firefighters were assigned a station off basic course, it took months before trust was established. That is the way it is and always will be.

Just as I informed everyone that dinner was ready, the alarms rang again. This time, it was a house fire in Paddington. As the two pumps and the rescue vehicle departed Roma Street it was common practice to send an extra fire vehicle from the nearest station to the fire and that was Enoggera. As we departed, my number two and I donned our breathing apparatus. As we entered Caxton Street near Suncorp Stadium previously known as Lang Park, we saw a small glow in the night sky and a plume of smoke rising straight up in the air. I had a quick chat to the station officer in front of the fire vehicle as we worked out our initial task for when we arrived.

As we pulled up at the residence, we saw a small section at the rear was on fire. I grabbed the case one hose from the vehicle, as my number two took the standpipe to find a hydrant. With every incident, your heart rate goes through the roof and mine was no different. The driver and pump operator fed me water from the tank on the fire vehicle. The station officer and I arrived around the back of the house to see only one room on fire. We climbed the rear stairs, but the back door was closed. I yelled out to my number two, 'bring me the Master Key, 'and he ran for the sledgehammer. In the meantime, we broke a window and sprayed the room with water. When he returned, we gained entry with one well-placed blow of the sledgehammer. In a few minutes the kitchen fire was under control.

We drove back to the station, cleaned all the gear we used, and tested it before replacing it back on the fire truck. As always, every bit of equipment on a fire vehicle is placed in a particular position. As a junior firefighter, I spent hours learning where each piece of equipment was and how to use it.

As the ladder crew had remained at the station, they kept the chicken dinner warm and ready to serve on our arrival. We sat down around the large table helping ourselves to dinner and talking about sports and what we did that day. The mood was cheerful as our crew had a few jokers on board. We always checked our equipment as we never knew who's turn it was to be the centre of a joke. As mentioned previously, some of the antics was black boot polish or Vaseline on head strap of helmet or honey in coat pockets or water in boots.

As we were cleaning up after dinner, the alarms sounded again, this time to the Premier of Queensland's Building. Being a high-profile building, this meant a three-vehicle turnout. As we entered the building, we were met by the State Government Security officers who informed us that contractors had set the fire alarm system off using a soldering iron, so it was another false alarm.

On returning to the station, a firefighter from each vehicle must alight to help guide the vehicle back into the allotted bay. The driver then plugs in the 240-volt battery charging cable to make sure it is always ready to start.

Around 2000 hours we were called up for a lecture on ship fires. After that, most of the guys made a cup of coffee and retreated to the television room to watch the 1980's movie "The Blues Brothers". We were all talking about their car, a 1974 Dodge Monaco sedan and how many cars got wrecked in the movie. A total of 104 cars were destroyed, when the bells rang out again. This time it was the Hot Gossip's nightclub. These were turnouts every firefighter hoped to be part of. This place was abundant with scantily clad women and firefighters walking in full turnout gear was a special treat for them. Often phone numbers and addresses were placed in pockets of turnout coats. I never knew anything about that, well maybe once.

Another false alarm. A toaster was the culprit. Smoke from burnt toast had set the smoke detector off. Returning to the station we made another cup of coffee and resumed watching The Blues Brothers.

It was approaching 2230 hours, and a few guys were retiring to bed to find they had been short sheeted. No one was left out, even the District Officer couldn't escape. But someone made a comment 'it feels like one of those nights' meaning we are not going to get much sleep. Most of us saw the end of the movie, we cleaned up the kitchen, made a cup of tea and then retired to bed.

Before we retire for the night, we leave our turnout coat on the seat of the vehicle we are assigned to and place our boots beside our bed with our pants over the boots with our braces open, all ready to go. As I checked my bed for any booby traps, the alarm bell went off again.

This alarm was at the Queensland Police headquarters. It was a short run and when we arrived, the security guard indicated it was a false alarm as a vehicle had struck a sprinkler head. Luckily it was in the car park and no damage was done. I radioed back to the watch room asking for a technician to replace a sprinkler head and reset the system. We arrived back at the Station around 0200 hours. I was getting very tired by then and looking forward to a good sleep. I placed my turnout boots and pants beside my bed, checked my bed again for any foreign matter, then laid down and fell asleep before my head touched the pillow.

An hour later, the alarm bells sounded and all the lights in the station came on. The place was like daytime. I automatically sat upright in bed half awake and half asleep, with my mind trying to comprehend what was going on.

Within a few seconds I realised where I was and what the noise and lights meant. My heart rate jumped from a sleeping rate to a high rate within seconds. It is a shock to the system that only firefighters can explain. I kicked my bedding back, slipped into my boots and ran to the fire trucks, while a voice over the PA system from the watch room said, 'A house is on fire, people are trapped, address is Lock Street Hill End Brisbane.' That situation meant a three vehicle turn out plus a backup fire vehicle from the nearest station.

As the fire trucks rolled out, sirens blaring and horns sounding, we donned our breathing apparatus. As we turned the corner and crossed the bridge over the Brisbane River, we saw the bright orange glow in the sky and knew this was no small fire. Then a voice from the watch room called again confirming a fifth fire truck was rolling and up to three people were still unaccounted for. This is every firefighter's nightmare, people trapped inside a burning structure. Our plan was that my number two and I would take the case one hose, try entry from the front, find the trapped people and rescue them.

On arrival it was a mess, onlookers everywhere, vehicles parked both sides of the narrow street and the house was well ablaze. It was mayhem as I alighted from the vehicle. My station officer called in a Code 02 then checked that my Breathing Apparatus was working. Our driver took the tag from my Breathing Apparatus and marked down my name and the time. I left the truck, and the same procedure was carried out for my number two. A lanyard was fastened to both of us as a safety measure.

The house was an old Queenslander with closed in verandas set high on stumps. I had to climb five stairs and walk up a steep incline before reaching the stairs into the house. As we approached the front stairs, we heard our station officer yell out, 'a woman and two young children are still in the house!' My heart sank but I was determined to rescue these people.

As I climbed the front timber stairs, the noise and the heat of the fire was unbearable. As I kicked in the front door, the heat was so fierce that we had to retreat back down the stairs. I was handed the case two hose line which had a larger flow of water and a lot more force. My number two pushed in close to my back, so I kept control of the fire hose and this time we made it through the front door. Later we found that both our helmets were warped due to the heat we experienced.

As I entered the house I looked up and saw the bright stars in the sky through the large opening where part of the roof was no longer. Communications between myself and my number two were impossible, but we knew what to do. As I moved to a new area, my number two kept an eye for any potential danger and if he saw anything, he would tap me on the shoulder or pull me back. I trusted him completely.

We entered a hallway and off to the left was a room. As we entered, I noticed a baby's cot near the wall. As I moved closer my heart sunk. I discovered a young baby lying in the cot, his arms and legs were pointing straight out, and he looked like he had an extreme case of sunburn. I shut off the flow of water, removed my left-hand glove and felt for a pulse. I was saying to myself, 'please god this baby is far too young to die, give me a pulse,' but the baby was gone.

We pulled the cot out into the hallway as this was a much safer area. As I pulled it around the corner, the bottom fell out and next thing I look down to see the baby at my feet with his eyes staring straight at me. Words cannot explain how I felt - I felt I had failed in my job as a firefighter. I covered the child with a blanket, and we continued looking for other survivors.

As we continued down the hallway, the smoke was thick, and our vision was limited to about half a meter. As we approached a large open room which looked like a lounge room, we moved forward about another two meters and I stopped as something in my head said 'stop, there is something wrong.' So, we retreated back to the hallway and entered another room. We found nothing in the room and continued back out through the double door to the western end of the closed in veranda. I noticed a bed in the western corner. In Australia they call these 'sleepouts'.

I looked around through the thick smoke and saw a small figure in a very strange position. As I moved closer, I saw it was a small child with his head imbedded into the fibro wall. The fury of this fire had caused the child to try and escape its reign of terror. He had run blindly around until he smashed into the fibro wall, wedging him and ultimately causing his death. His clothes were melted into his skin, and he was burnt beyond recognition.

At this moment we checked each other's breathing apparatus, and we only had another ten minutes before the five-minute whistle sounded, so we had to retreat back outside. I could not believe we had already used up nearly thirty minutes of air.

The firefighters outside were getting the upper hand with this fire, however the smoke was still thick and dense. I was drenched and covered in debris. At times I felt large amounts of water entering through the roof structure. I gathered it was from the telescopic boom on the second pump. I was so exhausted; my body temperature was very high, and I felt like collapsing. However, our job was not yet complete. There was still one missing person to be accounted for.

As we moved back out into the hallway, I decided to close our charged hose and leave it where it was as the flames were just about extinguished. Slowly we entered the hallway and continued back into the larger room, feeling our way along the walls. We made it back to the area where I decided to turn back because of the warning voice in my head. Now the smoke was clearing and there in front of us was a large hole burnt through the floor and on one side wedged in the hole was a charred lounge chair.

As I moved closer, I could not believe my eyes. In the lounge chair was what looked like a cooked side of lamb. That is the only way I could describe it. It was all that was left of the mother. Had I continued into that lounge room earlier that night I would have fallen through the hole and most likely had the chair, and its contents come down with me as well.

At this time our warning whistles started going off, so we returned to the entry door where we were met by a relief crew. I informed the substation officer and his senior firefighter of our findings, and they entered the house to retrieve our hose and carry out a further inspection.

As we re-entered the fresh air, the first thing that hit me was how cold it was. The street outside was filled with news crews, people and more fire vehicles, police and three ambulances. After removing my breathing apparatus and signing back in on the board, I was given a bottle of water by a kind little old lady. She asked me, 'how was it?'

I said, 'The worst fire I have ever been to.' Then I sat down in the gutter with water running down it, thinking about what I could have done different. It was 0400 hours now and I had news crews coming up wanting an interview. I got quite angry towards them, because they already knew of the three deaths involved. One journalist kept at me, so I turned around, and gave him a few select words. Thank goodness it was witnessed by one of our senior officers. The officer turned around and said, 'you deserved that, didn't you?' The journalist was never seen again.

I was escorted to an ambulance where I was found to have a fractured arm along with a large gash that required medical attention. I was taken to hospital and my arm x-rayed. It took 15 stitches to close my injury. To this day I cannot remember how or when this injury happened, I was that pumped with adrenalin. As I was being transported to hospital my mind was like a movie camera, playing over and over, repeating every second from when I entered through the front door of the house to when I sat back down in the gutter and started to recall my every movement. I kept thinking what I could have done better. Could those children have been saved?

As a parent or simply a human being, seeing a child injured is heart wrenching, but to see two children burnt to death and then accidently stepping on one and seeing his eyes looking back at me has haunted me forever. There's not a day goes by in my life that I don't think of this fire.

Chapter 7

Aftermath

As the ambulance arrived at the Royal Brisbane Hospital, I felt like I was coming out of a dream. Next thing I heard was the ambulance medic say, 'we have arrived at the hospital, keep your left arm against your body so you don't get the saline line caught'.

I looked down to see that he had inserted a drip into my left arm. My right arm was bandaged and in a splint. I asked myself, 'when did this happen?'

I was wheeled straight into the emergency theatre where a team of doctors and nurses were waiting. There was a lot of commotion going on as a nurse removed my splint and the dressing.

It was the first time I saw my injury and still I felt no pain. Next thing I remember was a radiologist asking me to place my arm in a certain position as x-rays were being taken, then another nurse appeared to start cleaning my wound ready for stitching.

As the doctor was stitching my arm, he got my attention and asked if I was ok. I told him what I had been through, and he said I had delayed shock, and everything would slow down in my mind in a few days after my body had time to compute everything.

As the doctor was putting the final stitch in my arm another doctor appeared with my x-rays. He told his colleague I had two fractures in my lower radius. I said, 'I need to get back to work.' The emergency doctor replied, 'you have just earnt yourself a holiday!'

'Can I at least go home this morning?' I asked him, and he agreed to that.

While the doctor completed stitching my arm, the nurse administered pain killers, dressed the area and before I knew it, my arm was plastered and a sling applied. As the nurse cleaned up, she handed me a piece of paper with a phone number on it. Being single and with what I had just been subjected to, I felt some happiness appear.

At dawn, as I was released from hospital, I still didn't feel any pain. The duty driver from Kemp Fire Station drove me back to the Roma Street Station. On arrival I removed my sling, walked in to see the duty officer and reported back. The clean-up of all the gear was still happening, and reports were still being written by the station officer.

I was informed that the district officer was present with detectives from Roma Street Police Station, and they wanted to see me. I was asked how I was coping before being informed that the two police officers wanted to interview me. As I told them what had happened, it all came flooding back. My emotions got the better of me and I broke down.

After composing myself I explained what I saw in the house as I moved from room to room. After my interview I reported to the Station Officer where we carried out a debrief and then I handed him a sick sheet for two weeks.

Everyone on B Shift understood the emotions we felt that morning. Being the start of our four days off and a

Saturday we all got together with our wives and girlfriends for a barbecue and a few beers. Another bonding session, but that's how the famous B Shift coped and looked after each other.

City firefighters are a special group of people because our lives are on the line every day. The trust and mateship we have in each other is paramount. We helped each other get over any traumatic events. Without the bond we had between each other it would have been much harder to cope with.

After that, I buried the incident as deep as I could. But it was always there. As I mentioned a few times before, a day didn't pass by where these types of incidents didn't pop up at some point in time. Things like that affect us even when we think we are 'over it'. A time would come when I would have to deal with it, but that was still years away.

For the time being, my resilience kicked in and I was able to continue my work. The reckoning would come later.

During my last five years as a firefighter, I saw a lot of destruction and loss of life due to the fires and road accidents I attended. After 1989, major changes were made in the Fire Act, and they introduced new building laws. These laws saw a major reduction in fires. During the end of this year, I left the fire service to move into the aviation world as a commercial pilot.

Chapter 8

On the Coast Watch

During my years as a firefighter, first in the Air Force and then in Brisbane, my wish was still to become a professional pilot. What I really wanted to do was fly, so as I was approaching the end of my nine years in the Air Force, I needed to make sure of that future. Waiting for my number to come up for pilots' school was a lottery I might never win, so I decided to apply for a discharge.

Within eight weeks, I was on a course with the Brisbane Metropolitan Fire Service. Once I completed that, I went to work at Kemp Place Fire Station. Working a shift of two days on and two nights on then four days off worked in well with my flying studies along with my part time job as an aircraft refueller. Having already obtained my Private Pilot's Licence I studied further to obtain my constant speed endorsement and my VFR night rating as well as my aerobatic rating.

After that, I transferred my training to Maroochydore Airport on the Sunshine Coast to complete my commercial subjects, including Navigation, Meteorology, Flight Rules & Air Law, Aerodynamics, Aircraft General Knowledge and Operations, Performance and Planning and even Human Factors. Then it was time to complete my commercial flight test.

I couldn't sleep the night before my exam. After my pre-flight theory test, I knew I had passed because otherwise I could not have proceeded to my flight test. I was told to prepare my aircraft to fly a customer out to inspect a station property. I had to obtain the latest meteorology reports and make my flight plan then complete a weight and balance on the aircraft. I was marked on every aspect of my preparation. One mistake and I could fail. I had to collect all my maps and the flight gear I needed to complete my flight. I was marked on how I treated my customer and all safety details. Of course my 'customer' was my Chief Flight Instructor. (CFI).

Arriving back at the Sunshine Coast Airport nothing was said as I put the aircraft away. I was very nervous as I was called into the CFI's room. He congratulated me on becoming a commercial pilot as he pinned a set of wings on my shirt. I was ecstatic with joy. It was like a pressure valve had just been released. I still couldn't believe that I was now a commercial pilot.

After a few days I came back to earth, as I now needed to complete my Senior Commercial exams, as they were called back then. I enrolled in a course in Sydney and studied these subjects through correspondence. After five months of daily study, I had my final exam on Performance and Loading. This is known as one of the harder subjects and it is based on flying the Boeing 727, an American narrow-body jet airliner.

By the time I became a pilot, it was the 1990s. In that decade, the dramatic economic and social changes of the two previous decades had changed how Australians lived. The internet took off and wi-fi was developed. Tariff protections were removed and that led to domestic businesses failing. The Mabo decision led to Aboriginal land rights and the Port Arthur massacre led to stricter gun laws. It was also crazy wild dangerous times of yoyos, chatter rings and Air Jordans. One could lose their eye or limb in a yoyo trick gone wrong.

I started my life as a commercial pilot with a job at Halls Creek, Western Australia for an Aboriginal Corporation. I remember the day clearly when the Chief Pilot gave me my wings and said I would start the next day. To gain a position as a junior commercial pilot in the 1990's wasn't easy as positions were very few and far between.

I had made a calculated choice on where I wanted to wait for a position to become available. The more remote, the better the chance. The competition was fierce to say the least. I was next in line for a position, but it could still take time waiting for someone to move on or get home sick. It wasn't easy living out in a one-horse town in the middle of summer with temperatures reaching +43 degrees. The heat was one thing, the flies were another.

Late one afternoon one of the aircraft failed to return on time. The pilot was a junior who had been employed for only two weeks before I arrived. He had to deliver food and goods to an isolated aboriginal community 250 km away in the Tanami desert. The only way you could navigate was using the compass allowing for wind drift and time over distance. Night fall came and now everyone was becoming concerned. Then suddenly, we heard an aircraft approaching from the south. The plane landed safely with about 5 litres of avgas remaining. He got lost on his return and that is a no, no. He was told to leave the next day, and I was asked to fill his position.

My time at Halls Creek was special because Kingfisher Aviation who I flew for was owned by the Wirrimanu Aboriginal Corporation. The Wirrimanu people lived in a very remote part of Australia at a place called Balgo Hills. It is situated approximately 1,780 km north-east of Perth. Approximately 460 people live in Balgo. Balgo is situated 250km from Halls Creek via the Tanami Track.

The most famous tourist site near Balgo is the massive Wolf Creek meteorite crater, the second largest in the world. To walk around the crater is a special experience but to fly around the inside of the crater was even more special. Wolf Creek Crater measures roughly 880 meters (2,890 feet) in diameter, and the mostly flat crater floor sits some 55 meters (180 feet) below the crater rim and some 25 meters (82 feet) below the sand plain outside of the crater. Geologists have estimated that it formed some 300,000 years ago when a meteorite weighing more than 50,000 metric tons struck earth at an estimated speed of 15 kilometres (9.3 miles) per second.

Of course, Wolf Creek is also famous because of the movies produced at the crater. The actual film was shot mainly around Hawker and Quorn in the North Flinders Ranges in South Australia.

It was during this time that I married for the second time and had two more children. Unfortunately, this marriage did not last much longer than the first.

Another company I worked for was East Coast Air, where I flew Queen Airs, a large aircraft with twin horizontally apposed eight-cylinder piston engines. Night air freight was their main role. I flew from Mt Isa each evening to Townsville where I spent the night and returned to Mt Isa early the next morning. It was on one of these return flights and about ten minutes out of Cloncurry I noticed a strong smell of fuel. First thing I looked at were my fuel gauges and I got a fright when I saw that the left-hand fuel gauge was very low.

I went through my flight plan and the fuel load that I had signed off in Townsville and everything else looked fine. However, I had this fuel smell which was starting to burn my eyes and getting much stronger on the flight deck. I knew by now I had a major problem, and I was somehow losing fuel from the aircraft. I contacted Mt Isa Control Tower and informed them of my emergency and declared a PAN: 'Possible Assistance Needed'. I wanted to hold as much height as I could before I started my descent into Mt Isa. I was given an emergency clearance for a straight in approach, so five minutes out, I started a steep descent. I landed the aircraft and shut it down immediately on the main runway. With emergency vehicles approaching, I exited the aircraft through the rear door.

After a safety inspection by the emergency services, the aircraft was towed back to the maintenance hangar where it was inspected again.

The problem was found to be a five-dollar washer that had ruptured in the fuel selector valve. This allowed the raw fuel to flow into the left- hand wheel well then past the outlet of the large exhaust at the rear of the well. The head maintenance engineer told me that the aircraft should have caught fire and exploded mid-air, as he had witnessed the same problem in Port Moresby.

I faced another problem one evening while flying from Mt. Isa to Brisbane. I was just north of Barcaldine and the area was deeply imbedded in thunderstorms when my left-hand engine shut down. I carried out emergency procedures and immediately contacted Air Traffic Control informing them of my emergency. They asked my intentions, and I advised them I was planning to land the aircraft back at Longreach airport.

The weather was turbulent, throwing the aircraft around and making it difficult to control the plane on one engine. I was sinking at a rate of 500 feet per minute. It wasn't until I reached 4000 feet that I could maintain height. Just south of Longreach I broke out of the storms and could see the airport in the distance. I positioned for a straight in approach and landed the aircraft without a problem. On inspection, they found that the inlet valve in number eight cylinder had dropped, causing the engine to fail.

Over the next ten years I flew for several companies and held Chief Pilot approval for two of them. Then I applied to Cape York Air in Cairns for a position in the Torres Strait. Cape York Air had one of the contracts to operate out of Horne Island. About five weeks after applying I had a call from the Chief Pilot who asked a few questions to do with flying in bad weather and instrument approaches and then offered me the job. I arrived in Cairns three weeks later and was endorsed on a Britten-Norman Islander. It had a range of 1,400 km, wingspan of 15 meters, and a top speed of 272 km/hr.

I was based on Badu Island in the Torres Strait where I could taxi the aircraft right up beside my house after the last flight of the day. The Torres Strait is a narrow band of water between Australia and Papua New Guinea. Throughout the Torres Strait there are about 274 small islands.

My job was to fly out of Badu Island every morning and do a pickup of the people from around 14 Islands then return to Horn Island to meet the Qantas Dash 8 from Cairns. I then took the passengers from the Dash 8 back home. I repeated the same flight again in the afternoon. Now and then I would do international charter work to PNG to places like Madang, Lae, Rabaul, Bougainville and Port Moresby.

On one of my return flights to Torres Strait, I had the Senior Pilot from Customs catch up with me after I touched down at Horne Island. He said I had been accepted for an upcoming position with Customs and I had to report to the Cairns base in two weeks. I let my Chief Pilot know and he said he had heard a rumour they were after me. He accepted my resignation and wished me all the best.

I reported to Cairns's base and the first test was to pass a flight instrument test on a flight simulator. Then there were a number of weeks of classroom and flight training before a final test. I was online flying between Darwin, Torres Strait and Brisbane. Mostly I flew around the northern part of Australia.

Sometime months later I was coming to the end of another tour of duty flying with Customs and I was planning a week's break back in Brisbane. The previous two months had been extreme flying with the summer weather playing havoc coupled with a lot of high intensity low-level flying.

We had some great success over the next months. My crew rescued a Torres Strait family who had gone missing for three days while travelling between Badu Island and Coconut Island to visit family. Travel by small boat is the main mode of transportation throughout the Torres Strait. It is quite common for boats to go missing up there because the T. I. people often fail to carry enough fuel with them. My crew also caught three illegal boats fishing within Australian waters as well as a boat carrying illicit drugs from Papua New Guinea.

We found a number of boat people while working in conjunction with the Australian Navy. We also found several small boats that were running drugs between P.N.G. and Australia's mainland. One of the greatest advantages was our FLIR radar which gave us the drop on any target. Our suite of communications included HF, VHF, UHF, Marine FM and Satellite communication links to anywhere in Australia.

Our patrol altitude depended on a number of factors, including the need to place a sensor at the optimum altitude and slant range for a specific target. The minimum height was 60 meters by day and 180 meters by night. Our main missions were to target illegal fishermen, drug and people smugglers and quarantine and environmental threats around Australia's 38,000 km coastline. A big job!

***

I got some time off and decided to go to Cairns. As I boarded the Qantas Dash 8 flight out of Horne Island, I was thinking of the great times I was going to have in Brisbane with family and friends.

Being based on Horne Island, we got to know all the various crews on the Dash 8 flights really well. In the lounge I was chatting with the captain, Brian, and First Officer, Peter, who I had known for about two months. We were discussing the weather because a Cape York Air Cessna had crashed due to bad weather only two days prior killing everyone on board.

Then Brian asked me, 'Didn't you fly with that company before transferring over to Customs?'

I answered, 'Yes, it was the last aircraft I flew before I left last year. Hadn't you better send the young fella out to kick the tyres and light the fires?' (a line I stole from Harry Connick Jr in the movie Independence Day.)

As Brian left to board the plane, he told me, 'You have a surprise waiting for you.'

When I entered the cabin, I was greeted by Stephine, a lady in her early thirties who should have been on the cover of Vogue magazine. We had a good friendship where Stephine would bring me supplies from Cairns and make sure everything was ok while I was flying in the Strait. For this trip, Stephine arranged a special dish for me as well as my favourite bottle of champagne. My usual seat was the last row on the left and, if possible, the seat next to me was always vacant. The privileges of being a Captain.

As the first Pratt & Whitney engine started to turn over, I was going through the start sequence in my head. The engine core needs to spin at 14% of its maximum speed before the igniters start. The engine core speed is called N2 and is expressed as a percentage of maximum RPM. On an ERJ, 100% N2 is roughly 16,000 RPM, so the engine needs to reach 2,200 RPM before the igniters start firing. Then I thought *I am on holidays; I am not flying this aircraft.* As we taxied out, the weather was quite bad as a storm cell was approaching from the East. I was sure the captain wanted to get airborne as soon as possible and head south away from the cell.

When we were airborne, the aircraft shook and rolled as the turbulence was at its worst. As we gained altitude at a maximum rate of climb, we were soon out of the bad weather and heading south on track. As the seat belt light was turned off, the cabin crew started to deliver meals and drinks. Being a Friday, it is usually a busy flight, but the plane was half empty. I thought, *that is good for me,* as the rear of the plane only had a few passengers.

Stephine delivered my meal - Scotch fillet and roasted vegetables - with a glass of Dom Perignon champagne, my favourite. She was a true champion and a lady of class.

As the aircraft passed abeam Coen, a small town in the middle of Cape York, Stephine sat down beside me, and said, 'I have a surprise for you. I am coming to Brisbane with you. We can spend the weekend together.'

I thought how wonderful this was going to be. As aircrew it is impossible to ever have a close friendship or a relationship as one or both of you are always somewhere in the world but never where you want to be and that is home. To have a weekend together was going to be special. We chatted some more on what we were going to do before Stephine flew out again on Monday morning.

The First Officer came over the loudspeaker and advised the cabin crew that we were reaching top of descent in five minutes. Stephine left her seat and started checking on the passengers. Soon after, we started our descent into Cairns Airport and arrived right on time.

I noticed it had been raining and storms were reported about for the day. Next thing I looked out the window and saw the wheels touch the ground. As the passengers were alighting from the aircraft, Stephine came up to me. She said she would meet me in the Qantas Club lounge in about 30 minutes as she had to sign off and get changed.

As I waited at the Qantas Club, I was thinking how wonderful it was to be spending the weekend with Stephine. But fate had more in store for me that weekend than just romance.

Chapter 9

Flying without a Parachute

After we arrived in Brisbane, we were met by our limo driver and driven to the Hilton Hotel. As we were having dinner, I had a phone call from one of my friends who parachutes out at Toogoolawah jump zone west of Brisbane. He asked me out for a barbecue lunch the next day, but I said, 'I can't. I am with a friend all weekend.'

Stephine heard the conversation and interjected, 'Let's go! I love watching the parachutists.' So, I told Grahame 'Okay, I am bringing a good friend.'

After we arrived at Toogoolawah, I was met by a few skydivers who I hadn't seen for some time. Grahame came up and asked me 'Who is the gorgeous lady?'

Soon after, I met the jump zone owner and chief instructor Dave McEvoy, who is a legend in the world of skydiving. He asked me, 'how are your hours going?' By that he meant, did I have enough spare hours to fly his aircraft?

We are only allotted a certain number of hours each month when we can fly. It's called officially 'Duty Times'. As I was having a week off, a few hours wouldn't harm my Duty Times with Customs.

I told Dave, 'I can do a few flights for you in the Cessna 182.' He was happy about that, saying, 'I have a four-way: three men and one lady practicing for the Australian championships in Corowa.'

With that, I gave Stephine a kiss and said, 'I will see you soon.' I went down to do a pre-flight on the aircraft. As I was checking the fuel levels, the team arrived and started to hop in the aircraft. I hopped into my seat, which is the only seat in the aircraft. The parachutists sit on the floor until we reach their jump height, then position themselves near the open door. I gave my radio calls and completed a pre run up and we were soon rolling down the dirt runway.

Once we were airborne, I set off to the east and slowly climbed to an altitude of 12,000 feet (3600 meters). As I contacted RAAF Base Amberley control to gain clearance, I noticed how cold it was compared to the aircraft I usually fly, which have heaters and are pressurised.

On our way up to jump attitude, one of the jumpers told me what position he wanted me to fly in on. I reached 12,000 feet and notified the jumpers we were commencing the run in. As we were approaching the mark, I opened the door beside me to the deafening noise of the engine and wind rushing by. The skydivers positioned themselves ready to jump and at this time the aircraft became very sloppy and sluggish to handle.

Just before they jumped, I pulled the throttle back to cut on the wind turbulence for their exit. However, in exchange for limited power, I was fighting with the controls to maintain a straight and level flight. As they moved outside for their exit, the aircraft became more and more sluggish, but suddenly, they were gone. The aircraft now became extremely light, so I immediately reapplied the power which gave me better control. I applied left rudder which takes the slipstream away from the right wing, allowing the door to fall into place. Then all I had to do was lean over to close the door before I commenced my steep descent.

The door wouldn't fall, so I tried again and again and suddenly out from under the aircraft flew a parachutist. I could not believe my eyes. The first words that went through my mind were: 'Houston, We Have a Problem,' the famous words spoken by astronaut Jack Swigert on the Apollo 13 spaceflight.

This was a serious problem and in those first few seconds, I didn't know how I was going to deal with it. So, I applied my three second rule. I developed this over the course of my life when confronted with all types of incidents. I stop for three seconds, gather my thoughts and then plan a rescue. If you dive in straight away, you could place yourself in harm and the outcome might be fatal.

There is a saying in the aviation industry that when a problem happens, 'Aviate, Navigate and Communicate'. I could still fly the plane, and I could still navigate and communicate. The only problem was that I couldn't land the aircraft as it would be certain death for the jumper caught up under the plane. My mind was racing trying to work out a plan of escape for the jumper.

I was only carrying 70 minutes of fuel plus reserves of 15 minutes. I didn't have long as I had already used 22 mins of motion lotion (avgas fuel) on the climb out. My mind kept racing to work out a plan of rescue. Having spent time in the military and the Queensland fire service, I was used to emergencies but with this incident, time was the critical factor.

After about a minute I had a plan. It was fraught with danger, but the only option I had that I could see working for both the jumper and me.

I had to make sure the jumper was conscious first. To do this, I had to unbuckle my harness and move to the open side of the aircraft to look out. A lot of parachutists have an automatic opening function. If they fall unconscious, their chutes will open around 3-5000ft. As I peered out of the aircraft, I could see that it was the female skydiver, Sue, who was caught by her clothing on the sidestep of the wheel strut. Her eyes were like cat's eyes at night being hit by the lights of a passing car.

I signalled to her to keep her hands away from her ripcord because if her chute deployed, we were gone. It would wrap itself around the tail of the aircraft and I would lose control and crash. That was not in my plan!

I returned to my seat and thought that I first needed to keep the plane in the area close to the jump zone in case she fell free. Her leg looked badly twisted if not broken so I wanted to make it easier for a recovery crew to find her. As the plane was being buffeted about due to the turbulence, I decided to place the plane in a very slight left-hand descent turn.

After I trimmed the aircraft to hold the descent, I retrieved a small knife from the plane's glovebox, slowly leaned a half a body length out the open door and started cutting Sue's clothing free. It was then I realised I wasn't wearing my parachute. During the take off, the parachute had been forgotten. This didn't faze me as the main aim of the rescue was to get Sue free so I could land the aircraft safely.

I decided that if I could not cut her free by 5000 feet, I would power on and climb back to 6,000 ft, declare a May Day and head for the Brisbane River. There I would attempt a landing on the river with the Water Police and divers in attendance to rescue Sue.

Every time I moved in the plane, it would change direction slightly. There was a real danger that if a gust of wind caught the upper outside wing of the aircraft it could flip, and I could be thrown out. I moved ever so carefully, trying to cause as little change around the centre of gravity as possible. There was a handle near the exit door which I held onto at times. Otherwise, I gripped my right hand around the lower floor rail. Each time I leant out of the aircraft, it would change its centre of gravity and roll around its longitudinal axis.

Moving slowly was all I could do to stop the aircraft from flying out of control. This is one of the reasons I placed the aircraft in a left-hand descent because the open door was on the starboard side, the side on which Sue was hung up. The other reason was it meant the aircraft was raised on this side and it gave me a slightly safer area to operate in. If the plane rolled, I hopefully would be thrown back into the aircraft rather than out of it. This was my theory anyway.

This aircraft had no autopilot, so each time it started to go into a slightly deeper pitch angle, I had to return to the controls to readjust the trim slightly then slowly return to my rescue mission. This must have happened over twenty times throughout the rescue. The gods of weather must have been on my side this day as the wind gust disappeared during the time I was trying to free Sue.

Every time I leaned out the door, I could see the horror on Sue's face. This made me determined to succeed. There was no way I was going to let her die.

As we flew over the jump zone, I could see the people below gathering on the airfield, watching what was unfolding. With each stroke of the knife, I tried to cut through more of the jump suit to free Sue, before again returning to the controls to correct the aircraft's descent. Over and over, I returned to the open door to continue my mission then back to the controls again, always checking on my altitude. When I saw that the aircraft was approaching 6000ft, I knew that I had only minutes remaining to release Sue. Otherwise, her parachute could automatically open on reaching 5000 feet, causing a catastrophic outcome for us both.

Two more times I remember returning to the aircraft controls and then with one more cut with the knife, Sue was freed. Quickly I returned to my seat and fastened my harness before tipping the plane over on a steep angle to see that Sue's chute had deployed. With great joy, I started my long downwind leg for my landing back on Terra Ferma.

On my descent I remember shaking like I have never done before as the realization of the event hit home. As I approached the runway, it felt like my first solo landing. I was thinking, *am I going to land this aircraft safely or am I going to crash?*

As the wheels touched down and I rolled down the dirt strip, I turned off and came to a stop near the pickup area. I could see plenty of people starting to gather around where I stopped the aircraft. As I shut the plane down, they all started to come over to me. Among them was Sue, running with a very bad limp. On reaching me she gave me the biggest hug and wouldn't let go until we were broken apart by friends.

Stephine grabbed a hold of me and gave me the biggest and longest kiss I think I have ever had. All I remember then was gasping for air, then hearing her say, 'you are a hero!'

I was asked to refuel the aircraft and do one more flight. The reason behind this was so I would not lose my nerve for flying. It was the best thing I could have done.

When I returned from that flight, I completed the maintenance release on board the aircraft before returning to the office to help Dave fill out an incident report. After completing the report, I was summoned to the entertainment area for a celebration and lunch. I was greeted by a large jug of beer which I had to scull as this was the first time this type of incident had ever happened in Australia or, in fact, the world. Sue came over on crutches and with her leg bandaged as she had just returned from the hospital. She bought me another jug of cold beer.

We sat down and went through the whole flight again, recalling both of our experiences that afternoon. I explained to Sue the things that were going through my mind after I saw her fly out from under the aircraft. The plan I quickly put together to rescue her and plan B if my first idea didn't work. I asked her about her automatic altitude release, and she said she did have one, but it was set for 3500 ft. Sue was very frightened that I would go below that height and the chute would open.

Everyone was buying me a beer, congratulating me and asking what I did up there to release Sue. I can't recall an afternoon going so quick and next thing I remember; darkness had set, and the Saturday night festivities had started. A Saturday night at the Toogoolawah jump zone is a night you will never forget. There was music, food and drink and it wouldn't be a Saturday night without Dave McEvoy playing his saxophone. I was that pumped with adrenaline I felt like I was floating all night until I went to bed around one am.

I woke up to a lovely breakfast of bacon, eggs and tomato prepared by Stephine. Around 0930 hrs we were saying our goodbyes to everyone as another aircraft was taking off. As Steph and I drove back to the Hilton hotel I still felt like I was floating on air.

We decided to go for a seafood lunch at the Hilton. My parents arrived soon after and joined us for lunch. Stephine soon was busy telling them what a hero their son was in rescuing this skydiver who had been caught up under his aircraft.

After our meal, we decided to go for a game of chance at the Treasury casino. My mother always liked a flutter, so I gave her $100 and said, 'good luck' With that I decided to try my luck at the one arm bandits. Stephine chose a certain poker machine because she liked the colours. After playing the machine for about 10 minutes, it came up a $1200 jackpot. With that we moved onto the roulette table and won another $300. It was our lucky weekend!

Chapter 10

A Belated Medal

About a month after the parachute incident, I received mail from the Australian Parachute Organisation. I opened it to find a Letter of Commendation for my efforts on that date. Unbeknown to me there was a further award I was supposed to receive but the whole Organisation caught fire one week later and burnt to the ground, destroying everything. The Australian Parachute Organisation then moved to Underwood, Queensland, on Brisbane's southside. After the fire, someone recovered three boxes of nearly burnt records. These were stored and not found again till 23 years later.

On going through the paperwork, someone discovered an application that was to be sent to Canberra for a bravery award. A new application was filled out and submitted to Honours and Awards in Canberra. One day in early 2013, I received a phone call from the Governor General's office saying I had been awarded a Commendation for Brave Conduct for my rescue of a parachutist back on the 4th of April 1993.

I was stunned that after all these years, I was going to be invested by the Governor General Quentin Bryce at Government House in Canberra. It was a great honour that winter's day to walk up to the Governor General and given an honour I had earnt so many years before.

As everyone arrived at the gates to Government House, security checked our licences and invitations. Then we were guided through a parking area to the front stairs where we were greeted and presented with our official invitations. My wife Debrena was led to the drawing room while I was led to a separate room with the other people receiving awards. Soon three more people arrived, and the doors were closed.

We were informed of all the protocol involved and how we must present ourselves when we were called up to be invested by the head of our nation. In the meantime, the official party was seated in the front two rows with family members seated behind.

We were guided to an area at the back of the drawing room where we were seated for the investiture. We were led up in threes and informed of our procedures and fitted with a clasp to which the medal or ribbon was to be attached by the Governor General. Before each person entered, the next person to be awarded moved to the entrance of the doorway, while the Governor General's secretary read out a brief on why the award was given. In my case I was standing at the entrance waiting while the secretary read this out:

'On the 4th of April 1993, Mr. Kevin James Hughes, while flying parachute sorties at the Toogoolawah Drop Zone, rescued a woman who was caught by her jumpsuit against the plane. After reaching the required altitude four jumpers climbed outside the aeroplane to position themselves for exit. One of the skydivers caught her jumpsuit on the aircraft step and was hanging upside down out of control.

Mr. Hughes left the pilot's seat and moved to the open door. As the plane travelled at 90 MPH, he climbed half a body length outside of the plane and reached down in an attempt to cut the jumpsuit free of the step. Between several attempts Mr. Hughes returned to regain control of the aircraft before he cut the woman free. The woman fell away, opened her parachute and landed safely. For his actions Mr. Hughes is commended for brave conduct.'

I turned to face the Governor General while she spoke to me. 'That is one of the bravest acts I have ever heard of.' Then she invested me with my commendation. I stood beside her as photos were taken by the official photographer.

After the awards were completed, the winners gathered outside on the steps of Government House for a group photo before retiring to the garden area for a party.

As my wife Debrena talked to the Governor General, General David Hurley approached me, wanting to find out more about that adventurous day. Soon we were joined by Mrs Hurley and my wife as we spoke about the incident. I remember General Hurley being asked by his aide several times that it was time to go. On two occasions General Hurley turned to his aide and said 'soon'. He turned back to me and said, 'I am astounded by your bravery Kevin.' It felt wonderful coming from a General of the military who in 2014 became the Governor of New South Wales and in 2019 assumed office as the Governor General of Australia. Hopefully one day I will return to meet General Hurley as the Governor General.

In March 2017 I received a phone call from Yarralumla, the Governor General's residence in Canberra, asking me if I would accept a Bravery Medal as my past award had been upgraded. I was stunned and excited. My wife and I would be going back to Yarralumla for me to receive the much higher award of 'Bravery Medal BM' by the now Governor General Sir Peter Cosgrove AK, CVO, MC.

This time I invited our good friends, Keran and Glenys, and my wife's friend Helen. Two Bravery Awards were invested on the day. As we assembled outside on the steps of Yarralumla to have our group photo taken, I mentioned to the Governor General I had last met him at Sir James Killen's 80th birthday at the Irish Club in Brisbane some years back.

One thing is for sure, Sir Peter Cosgrove has a memory like an elephant. He most certainly remembered! He invited me to stand beside him before the group photo was taken. Afterwards, he asked me if I had family here with me. When I said yes, he wanted to meet them.

As we walked through a side gate, Sir Peter collected two glasses of champagne from the waiter and offered me one as I escorted him to meet my wife and friends. It was another special day in my life and to share it with my wife and good friends was even more special.

Governor-General of the
Commonwealth of Australia

BE IT KNOWN that, with the authority of Her Majesty Queen Elizabeth The Second,

Queen of Australia, I have awarded the

COMMENDATION FOR BRAVE CONDUCT

to

KEVIN JAMES HUGHES

CITATION

On 4 April 1993, Mr Hughes, the pilot of a small aircraft doing parachute sorties, freed a
skydiver who had become caught on the aircraft step at Toogoolawah, Queensland.

For his actions, Mr Hughes is commended for brave conduct.

GIVEN at Government House, Canberra   By Her Excellency's Command
this twenty-fifth day of March 2013.

Official Secretary to the Governor-General

Chapter 11

Ghost Pilot

The turn of the century led to a lot of changes in Australia but at least the Y2K Bug didn't wipe us off the map. That first decade was momentous for me too, largely because of the fall of the two towers in New York, which changed life for all of us. The 2000's opened with optimism but soon turned to fear. Sydney welcomed the world to the Olympic Games in 2000 and Australia won a record 58 medals. The Centenary of Federation in 2001 was another opportunity to celebrate. But also in 2001, with the September 11th terrorist attacks, years of fear and racial tension followed.

The ANZAC Bridge in Sydney was opened. The Space Shuttle Atlantis was the first to dock with the Russian MIR Space Station. Steve Fossett became the first person to make a solo flight across the Pacific Ocean in a hot air balloon. In Australian Tennis, Andre Agassi won his first of four Australian titles. Pay television arrived in Australia. But the terrible Port Arthur massacre also eventuated, with 35 people killed and 21 injured, leading to massive changes to Australian gun laws.

From 1995 to 2002, I worked for two companies where I was employed as Chief Pilot. However, I also needed to gain senior management experience in the airline industry as experience in this area is highly regarded if I was to gain a position with one of the world's top commercial airlines.

A new company was looking for a chief pilot to help set up Southern Airlines which was going to enter the Regular Public Transport arena. They were leasing four Beach 1900 turbine aircraft which they were planning to use on a standard flight route between Archerfield – Ballina – Port Macquarie – Newcastle. I was interested but unfortunately, the tender never eventuated. This is what happens with the airline industry. It can be very cutthroat.

Within two weeks I was working as Chief Pilot for another airline. They had a Regular Public Transport run between Tamworth, Armidale and Brisbane Airport. They flew Metro's (Twin Turbine Aircraft) three return trips daily.

I flew as much as possible while also carrying out check and training duties as Chief Pilot. In winter the flying became very marginal around Armidale with low cloud levels. This meant carrying out an instrument approach using the on board Non- Directional Beacon (NDB Approach). This is a standard approach pattern you must fly that has been specifically worked out by the Civil Aviation Safety Authority (CASA). These are worked out using height and speed restrictions.

Once you turn onto finals there is a minimum you can fly to and if you are not visual you have to carry out a missed approach. The airline had a policy to carry out two approaches and if you didn't get visual on your second approach you would fly onto the next town. Most of the time, after reading your preflight weather report, you would have some idea if you were going to get visual before the missed approach height.

Unlike Armidale, flying into Tamworth was usually no problem as the major airlines were constantly flying in and out, so we would be regularly updated on anything unusual to do with the weather.

My job entailed a lot of paperwork and regular meetings with the aircrew updating them on new airline requirements, debriefs and aircraft maintenance.

I was gaining a lot of experience and by the early 2000's I started applying to the major airlines in Australia and around the world. Times were quite tough, and jobs were few and far between.

Then I received a phone call from a good friend who was in America. He offered me a job flying a Gulfstream V jet, the formula 1 racing car of the sky. This was about to change my life forever in more ways than I could have thought of. When explained what the position entailed and how much it paid, I couldn't believe it. 'Are you serious?'

All he said was, 'can you start by the end of the month?'

I couldn't resist such an exciting and lucrative offer and indeed was off to America by the end of the month. My first stop was Hickam Air Force Base in Hawaii where I started to obtain some of my clearances. This was my home for the next six weeks in order to earn my endorsement to fly a Gulfstream 5.

The G5 is a long-range, large and luxurious business jet produced by Gulfstream Aerospace. It flies up to Mach 0.885, (over 1000 km/hr) can climb up to ten miles high and has a range of 6,500 nautical miles. It typically accommodates four crew and up to fourteen passengers in luxurious comfort. However, I was told that the configurations in the G5's I was going to fly would be completely different.

Next, I was transferred to Cape Canaveral Florida. My first stop on the way was the Jet Propulsion Laboratory (JPL) in Pasadena California to complete my paperwork and identification papers. JPL was my ultimate employer in the scheme of things. I spent three days obtaining my clearances along with further briefings then flew with a Colonel 'Callsign Cheyanne' on a G5 to Patricks Air Force Base in Florida.

Cheyanne was a fighter pilot with the United States Air Force/ She had seen two tours of Iraq and two tours of Afghanistan. To say she looked like a supermodel was an understatement, but don't be fooled, she was as tough as nails and took no crap.

On our arrival, we received a greeting fit for the royal family minus the red carpet. We wcre escorted to Cape Canaveral in a 3-car motorcade and taken to a deserted part of the field to what looked like a couple of abandoned buildings - one very large hangar, the other an interconnected super two storey building.

As we arrived, a large hangar door slid open, and we drove inside. It was like entering into a new world: three Gulfstream jets, a Blackhawk helicopter, men walking about in sandy coloured clothing, not a uniform to be seen. The first thing I noticed was the planes had no markings at all.

After a debriefing, I was handed the keys to a new Mercedes car and escorted to my accommodation at Cocoa Beach, an exclusive neighbourhood area next to the Cape. I had a 3-bedroom fully furnished condo overlooking the ocean, containing every item you could think of including a fully stocked fridge and freezer. I had just unpacked and finished having a hot shower when my mobile rang, and it was Cheyanne asking me to be ready in fifteen minutes.

At work, she was all business. You would never pick this woman as a Top Gun fighter pilot, but she was just that – a very dedicated pilot who was going places. She never married and devoted her life to the military.

Her weapon of choice in the automotive field was a F430 Spider powered by Ferrari's 490 hp V8 which is capable of pushing the car to a top speed of over 310 km/h (over 193 mph) and covering the 0-100 km/h (0-62 mph) sprint in just 4.1 seconds. This lightweight and highly compact power unit produces a specific output of 114 hp per litre.

Waiting out the front of my condo, I heard this car coming down the road and thought, *this can't be*, but yes it was - all $195,000 USD worth.

Cheyanne was a different person after hours. She enjoyed the company of her friends, some of whom were A-list celebrities. This night, she said 'do you like comedy?' I answered, 'I am Australian. We have some of the finest comedians in the world, like Carl Barron and of course Hughsey.' (Dave Hughes)

Cheyanne told me, 'We are going to Gregory's Upstairs Comedy Club. I have some people I would like you to meet'. Being a Saturday night Coco Beach was pumping as we drove down the main road to Gregory's.

Cheyanne had a table reserved and some friends were coming. Mysteriously, she said, 'I would like you to meet some people who I am sure you will know'. I was thinking, *who would I know over here? I have just arrived.*

She introduced me to some amazing people who it turned out, I had heard of. I met Marg Helgenberger, an actress who starred in the Vietnam war series 'China Beach' and in CSI. Next was David Caruso from Hill Street Blues and CSI, then Gloria Estefan, famous for the Miami Sound Machine and the worldwide hit 'Conga' in 1985. The food was great too. I enjoyed eating a Jumbo Shrimp meal for entrée and a Surf and Turf for main course with a few glasses of excellent champagne.

Monday, I arrived for a 0730 start in our briefing room. After I sat down with a coffee, I was told we would be flying to Nellis Air Force Base for a few days training. NVG Training (Night Vision Goggles) would be conducted at a place called AREA 51, famous for UFO sightings.

Further low-level exercises would be carried out over the next month before I was fully qualified to mission status. Day and night flying was constant. This was extremely difficult at times, testing me to my limits and beyond. However, I believe if you want something bad enough you will succeed. Learning the ropes of my new position as a First officer on a G5 was not easy even with the number of hours I had logged in my logbook coupled with the flying experience I had under my belt. This was a new type of flying, which included both very high and super low altitude flying amongst other special operations.

I was fast tracked to gain my command on this aircraft. I was pushed to the limit and beyond every time I flew this sports car of the sky. The flying on certain missions was exceptional and other missions extremely dangerous. Being an adrenalin junkie, I found them exciting, where I would sometimes exceed the prescribed limits of the aircraft.

On standard missions there was an informal agreement that shuttle pilots could keep current by flying the G5's as well. It was quite daunting to be flying as a first officer when my Captain was an Air Force Colonel who had multi combat experience and was a qualified astronaut. The military people I flew with taught me so much about operational flying and it was this training that soon proved 'I had what it took' to become one of the newest members of this elite airline.

I met so many movie stars, international musicians, leaders of other countries and American politicians during this time. It was interesting, but to me everyone is just a human being - some were nice, and some weren't, simple as that.

Within a year, I was handed my command of the Gulfstream 5 with great fanfare. It was a time I will never forget. I was fast tracked and ticked every box along the way. I was held in high esteem by one 4 star General. I was quietly pulled aside by this decorated war veteran and told if I needed something urgently and I was delayed in receiving it I was to ring him direct. I was also given the rank of Major while I was employed with JPL. Then when I gained my command I was promoted to Colonel.

It didn't take long after I joined this organisation to understand what this operation was all about and why it was needed. After 9/11, the world was thrown into turmoil and the threat of terrorism was on everybody's lips.

Explosions were happening around different countries in the world; different terror groups would be blamed or take the blame. It was a time of massive uncertainty. America was dealt the biggest surprise and shock of their life when the twin towers were hit. Terrorism had entered their back yard, and it became personal.

So, the restraints on the CIA were lifted and one of those restraints was the relaunch of the CIA's Air America. The need for a covert airline to operate worldwide was necessary to transport suspected terrorists to various integration sites around the world, including Guantanamo Bay in Cuba.

Covert action was dangerous and if an American Agent was caught red-handed involved in an operation, he could be expelled or arrested or even killed. The field office and entire network and activities would then also be in danger, which could affect the entire operation.

The obvious solution to this conflict was to outsource the covert action, to use proxies for American power. One of the key advantages of using proxies was 'deniability' - the ability of the United States to deny any knowledge of an operation that either went wrong or became public. Another advantage of using foreign operatives was the knowledge they had gained in their various fields of operation. Because of this, they often required less training. They could also be disengaged after their missions were completed.

***

Extraordinary rendition explained.

Extraordinary rendition is a euphemism for state-sponsored forcible abduction in another jurisdiction and transfer to a third state. The phrase usually refers to a United States-led program used during the War on Terror. This had the purpose of circumventing the source country's laws on interrogation, detention, extradition and/or torture. Extraordinary rendition is a type of extraterritorial abduction, but not all extraterritorial abductions include transfer to a third country.

The administration of President George W Bush abducted hundreds of illegal combatants for US detention, and transported detainees to US-controlled sites as part of an extensive interrogation program that included torture.

Extraordinary rendition continued under the Obama administration, with targets interrogated and subsequently taken to the US for trial. A 2018 report by Intelligence and Security Committee of Parliament found the United Kingdom, specifically MI5 and MI6, to be complicit in many of the renditions carried out by the U.S. by helping fund them, supplying intelligence, and knowingly allowing the abductions to happen.

By 2004, critics alleged that torture was used against subjects with the knowledge or acquiescence of the United States, where the transfer of a person for the purpose of torture is unlawful. In addition, some former detainees, such as Australian citizen Mamdouh Habib, claimed to have been transferred to other countries for interrogation under torture.

Procedures in the 21st Century for transporting suspects

Following the September 11th attacks on the United States, the CIA has been accused of capturing hundreds of people suspected of being terrorists, or of aiding terrorist organizations in third party states such as Egypt, Jordan, Morocco, and Uzbekistan. Such ghost detainees are kept outside judicial oversight, often without ever entering U.S. territory, and may or may not ultimately be transferred to the custody of the United States.

Members of the Rendition Group follow a simple but standard procedure. Dressed head to toe in black, including masks, they snatch the prisoners, blindfold them, cut their clothes off, then administer sleeping drugs.

They outfit detainees in a diaper and jumpsuit for what can be an extended flight. Their destinations are either a detention facility operated by cooperative countries in the Middle East and Central Asia, or one of the CIA's own covert prisons, referred to in classified documents as "black sites" which at various times have been operating in ten countries.

Transport Services Aircraft

It was well known that a number of aircraft companies were operating as fronts for the Central Intelligence Agency (CIA). According to investigations, it was found these alleged companies did not have any offices or premises. Searches of public records for identifying information relating to each company only yielded post-office boxes in various states.

There have been several parliamentary reports made of various aircraft that were used to transport suspected terrorists to undisclosed locations for either extraordinary rendition or into the CIA Prison system.

A former CIA agent who was stationed overseas told me how it works. 'We pick up a suspect or we arrange for one of our partner countries to do it. Then the suspect is placed on your aircraft for instance and transported to a third country, where, let's make no bones about it, they are tortured. If you want a good interrogation, you send someone to Jordan. If you want them to be killed, you send them to Syria or Morocco. Either way the U.S, cannot be blamed as it's not doing the heavy work.'

I was not fully convinced of the rightness of these actions, but my views are only from my perspective. My mind flows back, thinking of the U.S Cole incident, the bombing of the U.S Embassy in Beirut, the bombing of the U.S. Marine barracks near Beirut Airport, and the Pan Am Flight 103 that exploded over Lockerbie in Scotland among others. In total the number of people killed during these acts of terrorism numbered in the thousands. In various countries around the world today we have a number of radical leaders who just want war and destruction. Unfortunately, we live in a world of uncertain times and the decision makers of our countries must deal with what is presented to them in ways of bombings on our homeland soil or terrorist related kidnappings.

Regardless, I chose to work in this job for many years. I did what I thought was right at the time.

***

When I was on a highly sensitive mission involving rendition recovery, traceability was to be wiped completely clean from every area of our mission. This meant that, if we were compromised or captured, nothing on our person, aircraft or cargo could be traced back to the US Government. We were contractors and after wheels up we were all alone, with no country admitting we belonged to them.

On each aircraft there were six to eight men, all dressed in black. After we touched down in a foreign country, on would go their black masks and gloves. Make no mistake, these missions were real, as terrorism is real. These men were usually retired special forces members from either the US Navy Seals, the Green Berets or a foreign agency such as the Special Air Service (SAS).

Our G5's carried highly classified and sensitive communications equipment. We could communicate with anyone anywhere in the world at any time. James Bond would have been jealous of the way these flying communication beds were constructed.

Before each mission we reported to a hangar on a specific airfield in a specific country where we would lodge our flight plans and discard anything that was personal or could identify us. We collected our passports, drivers' licences, specialized weapons and other personal items necessary for the mission.

We had entered another world, a world of high-pressure stakes where failure was never discussed. Even though I was part of a two or three-man crew up front, we were only the bus drivers. It was our responsibility to get the aircraft to its destination and then get it out without being compromised. The other part of the mission was handled by the men in the rear of the aircraft. These missions were highly sensitive and bloody dangerous.

We were in the world of retribution, flying everywhere to capture known or suspected terrorists and transport them to a Black Site in another country for interrogation. This was the world's way of retaliating against the actions of 9/11 even though these actions had been in force well before then. However, when terrorism hit the back yard of the US, it unleased a wild bear like nothing that has ever been seen before. I understand there were over 300 missions of this type carried out after 9/11.

I had entered a completely new world of intrigue, mystery and living a double life. I was now piloting a 'Ghost Plane', and I was right when I thought - *how my life is going to change*. Luckily for me, I was just the pilot – the jet jockey – so I had little or nothing to do with the actual kidnappings. Instead, I flew around the world living the high life - accommodated in luxury hotels, eating the best foods, and dressed in the finest Italian tailored suits. My role was vital to them, so they took good care of me. I will share with you in the next chapter some of the stories about those momentous years.

During this time, a year had gone by since I first arrived in the States, and I was informed I was being considered for a command on the G5. Over the next four weeks I made all the command decisions while being overseen by my Check and Training Captain. Out of the blue, after a six-hour mission he said, 'Congratulations, you have your command on a G5, and your rank is now elevated to Colonel.'

Chapter 12

Incidents Along the Way

We made a few flights into Bagram airfield in Afghanistan for various missions. Bagram airfield was originally built during the early cold war, at a time when the United States and the Soviet Union were both trying to influence Afghanistan. The original runway was built in 1976. Control of the base was contested from 1999 onwards between the Northern Alliance and the Taliban.

During the US-led invasion of Afghanistan, the base was secured by a team from the United Kingdom's Special Boat Service. By 2001, troops from the 10th Mountain Division shared the base with Special Operations Command officers from MacDill Airfield Base in Florida. The troops patrolled the base perimeter, guarded the front gate, and cleared the runway of explosive ordnance.

By 2002, Bagram airfield was serving as home to more than 7,000 US and other armed services. Numerous tent areas housed troops based there, including one named Viper City. It was reported that 'Bagram came under daily rocket attack' in 2002 even though a lot of these attacks were kept from the press for various reasons.

A second longer runway was built by the United States in 2006. By 2007 Bagram air base had become the size of a small town, with traffic jams and many commercial shops selling goods from clothes to food.

The base itself is situated high up in the mountains and sees temperatures drop to -29c. Due to the height and snowstorms commercial aircraft have difficulty landing there. Experienced crews are required.

One of our flights into Bagram airfield was around 0330 hrs in the morning late one November where the temperature was around -8 C on the ground with snow. The weather was very inclement coupled with severe wind shear on short finals. This made our approach even more difficult. We were delayed at our last refuelling stop in Scotland due to weather as well.

After our arrival I said to Cheyanne that we needed to check the weather again as we could see large storms approaching on our radar. We planned to have a two-hour turnaround as we needed to have the aircraft refuelled and my Artificial Horizon (AH) looked at by one of the engineers as well as a review of our flight plan.

We had to be on time because we needed to depart under the umbrella of darkness. Otherwise, we were a clear visual target to the Taliban in the sunlight. The plane was refuelled and checked and then we went over our flight plan that needed amending due to our late arrival into Bagram.

As one of the ground crew brought us a meal from the G5's oven, we were approached by the engineer who said he needed to take the AH to his workshop for some minor repairs. Both Cheyanne and I asked at the same time: 'how long is that going to take?' He said, 'I will have it fitted and working around 0630.'

I asked him if he could be any quicker. He said straight out, 'no!' I turned to Cheyanne. 'We are going to have to call in support for a daylight departure.'

Flying non-military aircraft out of a war zone with no fire capabilities especially during daylight hours is certain death by numbers. We needed an escort of fighter jets and helicopter gunships.

As morning approached, our aircraft was passed as serviceable. I had arranged for an escort out of Bagram for our southeast departure to flight level 490 (49,000 ft). Four Gunships cruised the area southeast of the airfield. We also had the assistance of an AWAC's Greyhound (airborne warning and control system) aircraft at high level above the Bagram airfield. These aircraft (E-2C Hawkeyes) are an integrated command and control battle management for surveillance, target detection and tracking. We were also escorted by five A-10 Thunderbolt 11 aircraft.

We did a final check of the G5 as our cargo of two Taliban prisoners (from the Salt Pit) arrived in black hoods and handcuffed with six guards dressed the same with black hoods and black gloves. The prisoners were secured in two rear seats for their flight to a new destination (Code name Cat's Eye). As we taxied, we communicated with the Bagram tower and our fighter support aircraft on a discreet channel indicating our Estimated Time of Departure.

As we started down the runway Cheyanne read out the numbers until the G5 reached V1 and she called rotate. We were soon airborne, and my eyes never left the screens in front of me. Straight away I checked we had a positive climb rate and increased airspeed. We were in a hurry to gain a maximum climb rate on our way to FL 490.

As we approached 6,000 ft a few minutes after take-off, a call came in from the Hawkeye indicating they had a threat within our departure zone. Immediately we went into our pre-planned escape route. I confirmed with Cheyanne as I put the G5 into a steep dive heading for the hard deck.

The Hindu Kush Mountain range can be unforgiving especially when it is covered with snow. Our emergency plan was to fly a pre-planned escape route through the valleys of the Kush mountains at 500 ft above ground level. We had rehearsed this many times on the flight simulator, but this wasn't a simulator ride anymore where if something went wrong, we could just stop the simulator and repeat the exercise. This was the real deal. Cheyanne said 'let's see if you are as mad as I am.' My answer? 'Hang on princess, for the ride of your life.'

As I levelled the G5 out at 500 ft, Cheyanne called out the numbers and directions like a navigator in a rally car. Next, we had communications from one of the A10's indicating we were being covered from above. We were receiving constant reports back from the AWAC's indicating our position and any enemy in our area. We had safely escaped. I was fortunate that this kind of incident only ever happened once during these types of operations.

***

Another incident occurred on our approach to Nice Airport. We were spending five nights in Monte Carlo on a crew break. We had just flown from Heathrow in London, a flight time of around two hours. Cheyanne and I had been pushed to our limit over the past couple of days and as our next mission was out of Malpensa, northern Italy, we chose Monte Carlo for our rest stop.

Cheyanne planned to meet friends who arranged pit tickets to the Monte Carlo Grand Prix. Being May the weather was amazing, dry and sunny. Monte Carlo was a river flowing with the who's who of movies, sport etc.

As we were approaching long finals I called "gear down". As the gear cycled down and locked, a single red light flashed. I informed the tower of our problem as we continued our approach and asked them to see if we had a wheel hung up. The tower confirmed we did. I asked the tower for clearance to make a left-hand turn out over the ocean to carry out further checks to confirm if we had a gear malfunction.

They cleared the aircraft for a left turn onto a heading of 155 degrees out to 35 nautical miles at 8,000 ft, squawking a new code of 7700. This is an emergency transponder code, so the aircraft is easily identified on radar. In the meantime, Cheyanne found the emergency procedures manual and started going through the section on landing gear failures while I positioned the aircraft.

Over the next fifteen minutes we carried out everything in our procedure's manual without any success. The only thing left was to try and shake the wheel free with some G-Force. This meant a sharp nose down attitude then pulling the aircraft up into a steep climb. This can force the wheel to shake loose and lock. After gaining a clearance we proceeded out to 50 miles from the airport and climbed to 12000 ft.

I told Cheyanne that I thought if we descended to 8000 ft, and I pulled the aircraft back up on a left-hand turn, the wheel should shake loose. She agreed but this took three goes before the wheel fell free and locked. Approach was contacted and we were handed back to the tower and informed them we required emergency services to stand by. Luckily, we landed without any further incident. The G5 was inspected, serviced, and cleared back to operational status.

As we left the airport I asked Cheyanne, 'where did you make a reservation for the next few nights?' She said it was down overlooking the water and I knew something special was planned.

As we pulled up along the Quai Antoine, right on the marina. Cheyanne said, 'here we are'. I asked 'where?' and she said, 'the Super Yacht you see in front of you'. I couldn't believe it. Who didn't that woman know? This lovely yacht was 40 meters long and had four decks. Propulsion was provided by two diesel engines driving two propellers. There was a crew of seven to eight officers and men on board to make it happen.

We had the most luxurious suites with full room service 24/7. All my suits and clothes were dry cleaned, pressed, and hung up in my clothes cupboard. I met some amazing people over the next five days/nights. One of the best nights was at the famous Le Casino Monte Carlo. Monte Carlo was buzzing with vibe and activity with the Grand Prix happening in four days. I really enjoyed watching the race!

***

One of our flights was carried out in late January from Los Angeles to Hawaii to Hong Kong and then our final destination, 4420 km away, in Moscow. We planned our flight time to be around nine hours. It was the middle of winter and conditions were freezing (-13 C) with snow falls predicted for our arrival.

We departed from Chek Lap Kok, Hong Kong's main international airport, which opened in 1998 replacing the famous Kai Tak airport. Anyone who has flown into the old Kai Tak airport will remember waving to the people living in their high-rise apartments as you were on short finals. It was one of the most technical approaches in the world but one of the most exciting for a pilot.

Our clearance for departure out of Hong Kong was for an initial climb to 5000 ft, then a further climb when instructed by Air Traffic Control. A minimum climb gradient of 4.1% until leaving 1400 ft was required and there was a speed restriction.

After departure, Air Traffic Control gave us a clearance to make a right onto a heading of 250 degrees, climb to FL 250 and await further instructions.

After we received our final clearance to climb to our planned cruising altitude of FL 480, we set the aircraft up for our 9-hour flight. I handed over to Cheyanne and went back to the cabin as I was asked to meet the passengers. All four gentlemen worked in Washington DC in the Pentagon and were big power brokers. We chatted for about half an hour over a few coffees before I headed back to the flight deck.

I checked all the engine instruments and asked Cheyanne, 'anything I should know?' She said everything was fine. The weather was 4 Octa's which in aviation terminology means scattered clouds. As we skirted the border of Mongolia the conditions below on the ground were freezing. Our outside air temperature was reading –62 C.

We were flying in the lower section of the stratosphere because you avoid the turbulence which is common in the troposphere below. The air up there is dry and contains very little water vapour. Because of this, few clouds are found in this layer and almost all clouds occur in the lower, more humid troposphere.

As we were flying IFR, (instrument flight rules) there are set flight routes you can plan your flight by. Along these routes there are reporting points marked by a longitude and latitude. (Example: GAYLE N 43'41.80' W 87'00.22') When you intercept this position you call the area frequency with your call sign, flight level maintaining and time to next position.

Fuel burn on these aircraft is exceptional. One of our previous trips from Asia to Alaska, we climbed straight to FL 410, then climbed to FL 450. We finished up at FL 470 and burned 33,000 pounds of fuel on a 11.5-hour trip. We cruised at Mach 0.80 until entering Canadian airspace then stepped it up to M 0.83 the rest of the way.

Before we commenced our descent into Moscow, we were hit with the most extreme clear air turbulence. This can be some of the worst turbulence an aircraft and its passengers can encounter. You cannot see this turbulence – it's invisible. We were being shaken around like clothes in a washing machine.

The aircraft fell 800 ft with no warning. Then suddenly, a warning light came on indicating we had a fire in the port engine. Cheyanne and I carried out emergency shut down procedures on the port engine and indicated to Air Traffic Control that we had an emergency.

A decision was made to carry out an automatic Emergency Descent and I contacted Area Control declaring a PAN (Emergency, where 'possible assistance needed'). When an emergency is declared Air Traffic Control gives the aircraft declaring the emergency all assistance needed.

After what seemed like an hour and a build-up of sweat, both Cheyanne and I had the aircraft back under control. I contacted our base back in America on our INMARSAT system. I had everyone scrabbling around with great urgency trying to find answers. I was told by our maintenance crew in America to land the aircraft and taxi to our normal hard stand, shut the aircraft down and contact them again.

I was given immediate clearance to intercept the 25L Instrument Landing System. I positioned the G5 on a 20 km final for runway 25L. Tower confirmed all emergency vehicles were on standby.

Having already configured the aircraft to fly on one engine, shortly after the engine fire shutdown, the landing was relatively easy, hence the long finals approach.

As we went through our landing procedures together and a few other scenarios if things turned to "shit, we were ahead of the aircraft and that's where every pilot should be, especially in an emergency.

We overflew the Outer Marker, OM, a beacon at or near the glideslope intercept altitude of an ILS approach. It is keyed to transmit two dashes per second on a 400 Hz tone, which is received orally and visually by compatible airborne equipment. The OM is normally located four to seven miles from the runway threshold on the extended centreline of the runway.

The G5 was performing perfectly. We were passing 100 ft with read outs every 10 ft until the aircraft's wheels touched the asphalt of the main runway. The G5 landed without any further emergencies.

I was cleared to taxi to the hard stand where we shut the aircraft down. I noticed the emergency services had followed us in. I gave an all clear to the tower letting them know we needed no further assistance.

The aircraft was made airworthy again in five days allowing us to continue our work.

Both Cheyanne and I were congratulated by all four officials on board, saying we would be mentioned for official recognition when they arrived back in America.

***

Not all missions involved cloak and dagger style operations. There were many other missions that were clearly above board; like collecting air samples over Alaska from a fire burning in Central Russia. We transported high level officials to meetings around the world and ferried well known celebrities to holiday destinations. They were serious, but they were also the cover for our real operations.

I was never contracted as a fulltime member of this elite team. I was simply used to do various missions and then to return back to Australia to continue my job there. It suited both me and my employer.

Australian pilots were always a favourite with the Americans for their flying experience mixed of course with the kangaroos and emus. Some still think kangaroos roam the streets of our cities on the east coast of Australia. Well, I did stretch the truth at times. How could I not, they loved it.

I flew on a handful of missions to various Black Sites around the world. Without divulging any countries involved I can use the covert names given to some of these sites. They were Bright Light, Detention Site Green, Quartz's, Detention Site Cobalt, Slat Pit, Gitmo.

One of the easiest airports in the world to fly into was Prestwick in Scotland. Quite a few pilots I worked with agreed that this airport was an excellent destination for refuelling stops and layovers. It was simply a place you could fly into any time and no questions asked.

Flying over Europe was easy as we were given a clearance to overfly. Some other regions were a lot more difficult.

The Gulfstream 5s were well maintained and a real pleasure to fly. They were planes that could never be traced back to the real owners. Registration of the aircraft would change on a regular basis as part of their covert roles. To those in the know they were simply ghost planes.

Chapter 13

End of the Line

The people I met, the lifelong friends I made, the journeys and adventures that I had were incredible for me, as well as controversial.

I suppose if I was to pick two of the most well-known politicians I met during that time, it would have to be the retired German Chancellor Angela Merkel and the 46th US Vice President Dick Cheney. Both were remarkable people and a privilege to meet. Two of the most colourful movie stars I met were Christian Bale and Kate Winslet. Both were very down-to-earth, funny, and loveable people. Three of the greatest sports people I met were Brian Lara, the Trinidadian cricketer who was one of the greatest batsmen of all time, Magic Johnson of basketball fame, and Michael Schumacher, the winning Formula One driver.

My flying career was cut short when I was having a break back in Australia. I was very fit at the time, going to the gym for two hours each day, six days a week. But one morning after my workout I ran up a flight of stairs and was out of breath. I reported straight to the doctors who sent me for an ultrasound, and they found I had a ruptured mitral valve in my heart. The report said I needed immediate open-heart surgery which took six hours.

Being so fit, I only spent four days in hospital before I was released into the care of my good friends Ivan and Aileen. It took me a few months to get back to normal after my surgeon repaired the valve. Soon after, my aviation medicals were withdrawn, which grounded me as a commercial pilot. This was a bitter pill to swallow.

I had a wild ride while it lasted and a life I would never trade. It proves to me that no matter where you come from, you can succeed in life. If you have a dream, you can either sit back and think about it for the rest of your life or grab that dream and try as hard as you can to turn it into reality. I'm not saying everybody succeeds but trying has to be better than just wishing. At the end of the day, you will know you had a go and that's got to be better than thinking – 'what if? If only…'

No matter what age you are, what handicaps you suffer, how poor you are or how busy you are, you can succeed. There is only one thing stopping you and that is YOU.

Sitting around each day even in my retirement is not a life, especially for me. Life is too short and the only way to succeed in life is to never stop learning. For me, retirement came suddenly and unexpectedly when I was diagnosed with heart problems and required open heart surgery. But I retired from flying, not from life. I still had a lot of adventures left to live!

I retired in 2008, and the world was changing. The Prime Minister of the day was the first PM to apologise to the indigenous people of Australia. Facebook was becoming increasingly popular, and it was normal to update your status more than once a day. Australia won 14 gold medals at the Beijing Olympics and 46 medals in total. The film "Australia" was released starring Nicol Kidman and

Hugh Jackman. And the age of mobile phones had arrived. Everyone had them!

After being admitted to the Prince Charles Hospital in Brisbane, having been diagnosed with a ruptured 4/4 Mitral Valve in my heart, I was seen by a surgeon rightly named Dr Hart. He examined me and said, 'You will not be leaving hospital till you have had an operation'.

I asked him how long it would be until I had my surgery. He said he was not sure, maybe a few weeks. I spent a month in hospital before I was informed that I was scheduled for my operation the following day.

By this time, I had witnessed a few cases where patients required further surgery as their previous operations went wrong. The result was that I was out of my mind worrying about if I was going to survive my operation, what kind of pain was I going to experience, and what other traumas there would be.

I will never forget the morning of my operation. I asked the doctor for an injection to help me relax before I was wheeled into the operating theatre. As I entered the theatre the first thing that hit me was the size and the lights and machines they had. The number of staff in there was amazing. I thought *it won't be long now* as I slid over onto the operating table. I was shaking with fear, not knowing if I was going to survive this five plus hour operation.

I feel that if I had been given an explanation in more detail as to what was going to happen then I might have approached the operation in a calmer manner.

Next, I had the mask placed over my face and a cannula placed into my arm. Then the white juice as I call it started flowing, and that was it. I was in the hands of the gods from then on. I was out of it.

Five hours later I woke in Intensive Care. I had a tube down my throat and had a number of nurses looking after me. All I wanted first was to have the tube removed from my throat. I just wanted to be free of the invasive tube and be able to breathe by myself. After the minimum time required, I had the tube removed. This was step one in my plan and it was working. 'Stay positive,' I said to myself.

I had a plan before the operation on what stages would happen after the operation was completed and with my positive attitude it was starting to happen.

Drifting in and out of conscious, the time passed quickly and next thing I knew I was allowed some ice to suck on. This felt like a major step forward. Then I was informed I would be transferred down to a ward in about two hours as I was responding very well.

Next thing my parents were allowed in to see me. Being an only child and knowing what my mother had gone through with her own open-heart surgery; I became very emotional. It felt like a major weight lifted off my shoulders and at the same time I never wanted to put my parents through this type of trauma, seeing their only child have major surgery.

I was transferred back to my ward later that day, but I spent only four days in hospital before I was allowed to go home.

Seeing my mother wasn't in the best of health, I chose to stay at my good friends' house where they kindly offered to look after me. Ivan and Aileen Ryan are the most compassionate people you would ever meet.

In the following days, weeks and months I recovered better than normal. My professional flying days were now over, and it was hard to accept, but I now had a job working for the Queensland Government as a security guard.

I purchased an apartment in Nundah which was about five km from the Brisbane CBD. It was very handy to work and was central to everything I needed.

Nearly every day I used to meet my good mate Malcom over in Anzac Square at the Coffee Club. Malcom worked for one of the larger air conditioning companies and looked after Queens Plaza in Brisbane. One day Malcom brought along one of his apprentices, Kris. This young fellow was very quiet, and I asked him, 'what coffee would you like?' Mal answered for him: 'he doesn't drink coffee'. I looked at him and asked, 'what's your surname again?' He said 'D'Alessandro'. I laughed and said, 'an Italian name and you don't drink coffee? So, things changed that day and Kris was converted to becoming a coffee drinker. After that, Malcom, Kris and I met on a twice daily basis for coffee and a chat.

The following week I had just arrived at work and was summoned to the Judges' private carpark as there was an intruder seen lurking about. I summonsed my good mate from upstairs who worked for Veteran Affairs as their security guard. We met in the carpark in the L3 basement. Working for Queensland State Government Protection we were given certain powers of arrest and detainment. As we met at the basement lift, I worked out a plan and then we went looking for this fellow.

As we were both looking inside and around each of the judge's cars, I found a man asleep on the front seat of one car. I called to my friend to join me. I tried to gain the attention of the man inside the locked car, but without success. Even when I started knocking on the glass with my telescopic baton.

I indicated to my friend we might have to break the glass to gain access. I radioed back to base asking for police assistance as we had a person who had trespassed on government property and committed a number of offences.

I tried again trying to awaken the offender by hitting the glass with my baton. This time there was movement as he became conscious. I identified myself to him and asked him to open the door. He wouldn't obey any of my instructions, so I tried again and on the fourth attempt he opened the door.

As I moved forward, I was hit by the strong smell of rum. It was very powerful and indicated to me he was intoxicated. I ask him to remove himself from the car a number of times without success, so I entered the car, being very careful of any weapons he might have in his possession. As I went to grab him, a fight broke out. The fight was intense where a number of punches were thrown and where I received a severe shoulder injury, bruising and bite injuries. I finally gained the upper hand and with the help of my security friend we were able to remove him to the outside of the vehicle where I handcuffed him and read him his rights.

I transported him up to the main foyer where we were met by two uniformed officers. We exchanged handcuffs and notes and then he was taken away to the city watchhouse for processing.

I attended the local hospital for treatment and then I proceeded to the police station to complete the necessary paperwork. That afternoon the offender attended court and was awarded bail to reappear at a later date. Unfortunately, he packed his bags and left on the next plane out of Brisbane for Africa, never to be seen again. There is a strong lesson for the courts here and that is to make sure offenders surrender their passports!

After that episode I decided it was time to totally retire from the work force as I was financially secure. It was time to enjoy the rest of my life travelling the world and finding that certain lovely lady I knew was out there somewhere for me.

Chapter 14

Looking for Love

Being a mature aged single, I was never one to go out to clubs to search for the love of my life. I suppose I was the shy type when it came to that side of things but there is no doubt I wanted love in my life.

One day I was at the Coffee Club in Anzac Square and at the next table was this beautiful lady sitting by herself. I summoned up the courage and said hello and asked her if she would mind if I joined her. To my surprise, she said, 'sure'. I introduced myself and my life changed from that moment on. Debrena is one of the kindest and most beautiful women I have ever met, and I love her with all my heart.

The fun we have had together has been out of this world. We went out for dinners, attended concerts, travelled interstate and overseas, all within the first few months of knowing each other. As they say, it was a match made in heaven.

A funny incident happened about two months after we met. Debrena surprised me by booking an apartment at Mt. Tambourine north of the Gold Coast for the weekend. This included wonderful dinners and lunches, as well as massages amongst a peaceful forested setting.

We watched a movie with a delicious spread of cheeses and fruit jams from the local area and two bottles of champagne set out for us. It was about two hours till we had to get ready for dinner, so I said, 'let me run a spa'. I dropped the complete contents of a bottle of bubbles in the water and went back to my champagne. About ten minutes later I heard something, looked around and saw a tsunami of soap suds rolling out of the bathroom into the living area. What a mess!

An extraordinary thing happened when I was invited to Debrena's place for the first time. As I entered her apartment, I saw her son Kris. I nearly fell over - he was my best friend Malcom's apprentice! No one could believe it. What are the odds?

Six months after we met, we decided to move in together. We just fit together so well, it was the right thing to do.

Valentine's Day was approaching so I secretly planned a romantic holiday to Fiji. I booked two return flights to Nandi with Virgin Airlines. We had already planned a holiday, but she wasn't going where she thought she was going!

Debrena used to own a travel agency and understood what the term 'dead leg' means. This is when an international flight arrives at an international terminal and then continues on an internal flight. So, I said I was planning a holiday to Cairns, and that we had to pick up a dead leg from Brisbane International Terminal to get there.

The planning was so covert that Debrena didn't have a clue what was really happening. The night before, I secretly packed her passport. All the tickets were arranged and the airline staff at the airport were in on it, in order to help me with the subterfuge as long as possible.

It was the day before Valentines Day when we arose early to catch a taxi to the airport. It was pouring with heavy rain as it had been all night. As we arrived at the foyer a stretched black limousine was waiting. The driver greeted me and said, 'your car is ready Mr Hughes'.

After our bags were stowed away the driver helped us with umbrellas due to the continuing rain. Debrena was so surprised by the limo and even more so when she hopped inside and saw the champagne on ice for our trip to the airport. As we consumed a vintage bottle of Dom Perignon Champagne, Debrena talked excitedly about her next few days in Cairns.

As we approached the check-in desk, the airline representative said 'welcome Kevin and Debrena for our flight to Cairns'. I still do not know how Debrena didn't pick up on where this flight was really going but she soon got the picture when, as we proceeded through customs, the officer asked for our passports. Debrena was completely stumped. With that I produced our passports. She asked, 'what is going on?' and I replied, 'we are off to Fiji'. She was thrilled, dumbfounded, and amazed that I had pulled this off.

After we arrived, we were driven to the Sofitel Fiji Resort. I had a secluded table booked for dinner with a delightful choice of seafood to be served with some excellent wine. As the night progressed, I couldn't wait until Valentines Day. I produced an engagement ring and asked for Debrena's hand in marriage. All I heard was 'yes, yes, yes'. Being old fashioned, I had asked her son's permission first and he was all for it. It was a holiday we will never forget.

Later that year, we travelled to Europe for a six-week pre-wedding honeymoon. After stopping in Hong Kong, we flew to Rome, where we visited all the sights.

From Rome we flew to Venice for a few days, then drove to Milan. From Malpensa we flew to Prague for four days. From Prague we flew to Prestwick in Scotland and visited my grandfather's hometown in Denny. After that, we travelled to London for a week then boarded the tube for Paris.

In Paris, I had arranged front row tickets at Moulin Rouge. A good friend I worked with in America was kind enough to arrange them which was another big surprise for Debrena. Before our limo arrived, I arranged for champagne and French chocolates to enjoy. It was a romantic evening all around!

The next morning, we had breakfast at a local café. As we were eating, a large explosion shook the whole restaurant. I looked around and nobody was moving with any urgency, but we heard sirens coming from everywhere. I asked the waiter, 'is everything ok?' Calmly he replied, 'oh there must have been a gas explosion a few doors down'. Next thing the fire brigade was running around with hoses going everywhere and blocking the front door. I thought about how differently things were done in France.

After we finished breakfast the fireman near the main entrance opened the door for us. I walked through the spaghetti of fire hoses to have a look down the alleyway and just next door the whole wall of the building was blown out.

On our last night in Paris, we had dinner on top of the Eiffel Tower, with the city laid out in splendour around us.

Next, we travelled by fast speed train to Frankfurt where we saw a football match where Frankfurt played Hanover. An exciting game!

After that, we flew home to Sydney, but our travels weren't over. We followed Europe with a three-week cruise around the South Pacific islands. We travelled on the P&O ship Pacific Dawn with Debrena's best friend Helen and her three adult children.

Three days out of Vanuatu I was speaking to one of the crew who worked in the gaming area. She knew our story and suggested that we get married in Vanuatu. Her brother was the senior purser on board and could arrange it all for a small fee. I went back to our room and said to Debrena, 'I want to marry you in Vanuatu'. She wanted to know how. I told her the story and she said yes.

The ship anchored in Santo the following day and we purchased matching sarongs and tops. We talked to the purser, who arranged a pastor, two brand new Landcruiser vehicles with fresh flowers, a cameraman and a launch to Erakor island.

Debrena's friend Helen was bridesmaid, and her son Luke was best man. After we exchanged our vows, we signed the certificate of marriage. Photos were taken and then we had a small party. I had secretly arranged a three-tier wedding cake and of course, bottles of champagne. I had our room decorated as well. It was one of the happiest days in my life.

We have been married over sixteen years now and our love for each other has only strengthened. I would be lying if I didn't say we have our moments. However, we talk it out, then make up, which builds our love for each other even stronger. I will be the first to admit I am not the easiest person to live with, because I suffer from PTSD and depression.

The first thing you must do to have a successful marriage when suffering with this type of illness is for both parties to understand how this illness affects those around you and learn what the triggers are that can set the illness off. You have to be able to ask for help, then communicate with each other about how you each feel. It is very important to communicate your feelings for each other. Needless to say, it's also advisable to have a good relationship with your doctor.

On our arrival back in Brisbane, Debrena returned to work as a real estate agent. Over time we built up a small stable of properties and that worked out well for us when Debrena finally retired. As I am handy with my hands, I renovated the houses and then we rented them out before selling them to purchase other properties.

We both stayed fit by using the gym at the Tattersalls Men's Club. At the start it was a men's only club where women could attend as guests. This has changed now to include women as full members.

Vanuatu Wedding 2009

Chapter 15

The Next Phase

The next decade was a busy one for Australia. We got our first saint when Mary MacKillop was canonised by Pope Benedict XVI. Australia ended its combat operations in Iraq. Qantas flew the Airbus A380 for the first time. Aviation pioneer Nancy Bird Walton died aged 93. Floods hit North Queensland in a disaster that put about one million square kilometres under water. Massive wild bushfires swept Victoria on Black Saturday, killing 173 people, and destroying more than 2,000 homes. Anna Bligh became the first woman in Australia to be elected premier when Labour won the Queensland State Election and Nova Peris became Australia's first Indigenous woman elected to federal parliament.

In 2012 a certificate was finally issued stating a dingo killed Azaria Chamberlain. The National Disability Insurance Scheme (NDIS) was started. The High Court of Australia recognised non – specific sex identification. Aboriginal elders issued the Uluru Statement from the Heart. The International Campaign to Abolish nuclear weapons (ICAN) was awarded a Nobel Peace Prize. The amendment of the federal Marriage Act in 2017 gave same-sex couples got the right to marry. Bushfires continued to rage throughout Australia.

From 2010 onwards till Debrena retired in 2019 we travelled Australia and the world. Being retired I got bored and started a few small businesses to keep me occupied. I dabbled in LED lighting which was a new industry in Australia and still very expensive even though there were great electricity savings to be made. I specialised in LED street lighting and high-end flood lighting.

I searched companies in Shenzhen in China where I made the proper introductions and arranged my first meeting with them. In total I travelled to China eight times for business as well as Hong Kong seven times, Taiwan four times and the Philippines five times.

I met lots of wonderful people, including two men, Anthony and Bingo, who became close friends. I asked Bingo one day 'why did your mother call you Bingo?' He said, 'because it is lucky'. I couldn't argue with that. The two men took me out to dinner whenever I went to China, and they never let me pay. No argument was allowed, and the food was always excellent.

The products were second to none. After gaining the licences to have the lights approved under Australian Standards, I made quite a few government contracts. One was the relighting of the Bowen Wharf with specially designed lighting so it will not interfere with the mating season for the Loggerhead turtles. At the time this was a breakthrough in Australia.

I was fortunate to visit most parts of China including the Great Wall, Forbidden City, Zhangjiajie National Park, Tiananmen Square, Shanghai, Beijing and many other places including the famous Terracotta Army in Xian in the Linting District in Northwest China.

The terracotta figures, dating from the late 200s BCE were discovered in 1974 by local farmers in Linting County, outside Xian, Shaanxi China. The figures vary in height according to their rank, the tallest being the generals. In total, the three pits containing the Terracotta Army hold more than 8,000 soldiers, 130 chariots with 520 horses, plus another 150 cavalry horses. It was an amazing sight to see.

I invited Bingo to Australia a few years ago as we had a contract with one of the major councils in trialling the new LED streetlighting. I took this opportunity to travel around Australia with Bingo to introduce him to various government and council heads.

Having retired at an early age I didn't want a business that took most of my time. I just needed something to keep my mind ticking over and I found interesting to work on. The lighting business was starting to suck up more time each month as it grew, and it became a thorn in my side. The money was secondary, and I was having to spend too much time away interstate and overseas. I decided I was at the wrong end of the scale for this pressure. With that, I sold the contracts off where the manufacturers guaranteed further sales by the new owners.

We were much happier after that because we could go away or down to a coffee shop or out to dinner any time we wanted, without the commitment of having to be somewhere in the world at a specific time.

Bingo and Anthony and their wives, both named Joy, are still good friends of ours and we speak regularly on the phone. The thing I miss the most though is the authentic Chinese food. It is very special.

Debrena eventually left her job with her brother's real estate agencies and ventured into commercial real estate. This meant setting up and operating brand-new high rise commercial and residential buildings. This was a great challenge for Debrena. She is a woman that always wants a bigger challenge in life. She developed sets of operational and emergency procedures and gained the various approvals needed. Her details to perfection and six sense was spooky at its best.

Managers and workmen often thought a woman was an easy target - until they met Debrena. She was fair and by the book but do not try to pull the wool over her eyes! That was fraught with danger. I have never seen anyone so able to read a person's makeup after talking to them for a short period of time. She had this special gift.

We travelled Queensland and managed several high rises and large commercial properties. We met a lot of interesting people and made some wonderful friends. My favourite place was Port Douglas. It's a tropical paradise with wonderful restaurants and some of the best fishing in the world.

Port Douglas is also on the doorstep of one of the World Heritage Listed Great Barrier Reef. It gave us the best of both worlds. Debrena managed a 200 bedroom resort with one of the largest pools in any Australian resort. It backed on the famous Sheraton Mirage Resort where we became friends with the head manager and his lovely wife. We had some amazing times wining and dining and being introduced to many celebrity visitors.

I bought a boat because I love fishing. Having spent time in the Torres Strait, I knew what to expect and the wonderful species that can be captured. The local tackle shop in Port Douglas was helpful and had a great supply of fishing gear. I was soon asked to go fishing with them so they could share some of their favourite fishing spots. One Friday afternoon, Sam, who worked in the shop after school, offered to show me some interesting spots. He said he would have all the gear. All I had to do is turn up.

As we launched the boat at the famous "Tin Shed" it was always a necessary to spend the least amount of time in the water and place the boat between the inlet and yourself. Why, might one ask? Very simply there are some very large crocodiles that call the inlet home. Every day you would see a crocodile sunning itself or floating down the river.

Our type of fishing for this session was lure fishing. This meant tying a special lure on the end of your line and casting it out into the water and winding it back in with jerking motions. We covered a lot of area and were always on the lookout for movement in the water or jumping bait fish.

By the time night had fallen, we were slowly working our way back up the inlet. We noticed in the distance a group of trawlers had pulled up near Marano's Fuel. This is a T shaped concrete jetty where the trawlers back in and tie off. This time they had their flood light shining onto the water closest to the shore. This attracted heaps of bait fish and with the bait fish came large schools of the famous Australian fish, the barramundi. They were smashing the bait fish schools and were exceptional size. As we positioned the boat and lowered the anchor, we cast our lures and instantly we had a double hook up. We lost a few fish that night but landed six quality fish between us, the biggest being 857 mm long. We could have kept fishing however we only take what we need and so left the fish for another day.

Another memorable trip was when I took my friend Tony out from Port Douglas to the now famous "Batt Reef". That is where the Crocodile Hunter Steve Irwin was attacked by a large stingray and died in 2006.

My boat length was 4.2 meters - not an ocean liner by any means! Safety is always paramount in my operations. I had the latest in GPS equipment and carried two EPIRB's, first aid equipment and life vests. If something happened, we would be rescued. The Coast Guard always knew where we were as I radioed my position regularly.

The weather for the day of our trip was perfect. The water was smooth with a strong tidal drift to the north-west, clear skies with 2-3 knots of breeze till after 1500 hrs increasing to 8-10 knots. By this time, we would be well and truly on our way home.

As we launched the boat at The Tin Shed in Port Douglas, I had everything in its place and set out for our 34 km trip to Batt Reef. By the time we reached the 18 km mark the lights on the mainland had disappeared and we were in complete darkness until daylight broke some 30 minutes later.

After daybreak it wasn't long till we were approaching the edge of the reef. I will never forget it. One second, we were in 90 meters of water and next we were in six meters - the edge of the reef rose that quick. It was an amazing sight being out in the middle of the ocean with crystal clear aqua blue water where you could see the magical reef structure all the way to the bottom.

No sooner had we cast our lures and set up to troll, we had one reel screaming with a decent fish on the other end. After a fight of fifteen minutes, I landed a nice Red

Emperor which is an excellent table fish. We ended up with eight decent fish that day.

I used to compete nationally in fishing competitions in the light line class of 1 – 2 kg. This meant catching the biggest fish and landing it on a one or two kilo line. Each fish is given a fighting factor, and the points worked out on the line class. I still hold several All-Tackle Australian Records, National and State Records.

I was heavily involved in fish tagging for quite a few years which was great for research and tracking the movement of certain species. Some of my recaptures by other fishman were quite amazing. I tagged a bass species in Somerset Dam west of Brisbane and the fish ended up going over two dam walls and was recaptured near Fernvale in the Brisbane River. The fish had been swimming around since I tagged it for over seven years!

During those years Debrena and I loved trying new restaurants wherever we go, and we have special places we always revisit when we can. Whenever I go to Sydney, I take the ferry over to Manly and order fish and chips at the café at the end of the mall. I love to sit on Manly Beach eating them and watching the surf roll in. I have similar rituals in other places I visit regularly.

New Zealand's South Island is one of my favourite places to visit during the Australian winter. The airfares are reasonable, the wines are in abundance, mull wine is served in all restaurants and ski fields, and I love trout fishing. Plus, you are only three hours from your destination.

People have often asked me, what is your favourite place in the world? I cannot answer that. There are so many wonderful places, each having their own charm. These are a few places I found special. The first is Socotra in Yemen. Socotra is an archipelago of four islands located in the Arabian Sea, where around 800 rare species of flora and fauna exist. Unfortunately, Yemen is a dangerous country these days, but I hope someday it will improve.

Cappadocia, Turkey, an area in Turkey where entire cities have been carved into rock, is pretty incredible. Another incredible place is Salar de Uyuni, the world's largest salt flat, located in Bolivia. The largest salt mine in the world is one its most beautiful wonders.

The Blue Lagoon is a geothermal spa in southwestern Iceland. It is in a lava field on the Reykjanes Peninsula and seeing it is an experience that will stay with you for a lifetime. Lake Baikal is also hard to beat. This massive high-altitude rift lake in Siberia is the oldest and deepest lake in the world. Lake Baikal holds around 20 percent of the worlds fresh water. The 25-million-year-old lake is surrounded by mountain ranges.

As you can probably tell, I love the water and am lucky enough to have visited some of the most amazing bays in the world. My favourites are New York Harbour, the Caribbean, and most of all, Sydney Harbour - the most picturesque of any harbour in the world in my opinion!

Some of the best restaurants I fell in love with during my flying days are as follows. I loved New York for the deli's, the rolls and sandwiches, especially 7 Brothers Famous Deli, not far from Carnegie Hall.

In France, go to Cancale, which means oysters. In fact, even the uninitiated would be hard pressed to name anything else about this little seaside town, which is just a short strip of excellent seaside restaurants and oyster stalls.

Dublin is renowned for one of the best steaks in the world at the famous Hzanahan's on the Green. The steaks are certified grass-fed Angus and cooked in a special broiler to pink perfection.

The restaurant Norma, in Copenhagen has the finest Nordic food in the world. It is famous for serving dishes featuring ingredients that are locally foraged from game-inspired dishes like reindeer to fermented rice ice cream.

In Russia, try the Chemodan restaurant in Moscow. It serves some of the finest caviar in the world and the meals are to die for.

Suffice to say, I love good food almost as much as I love the water.

Chapter 16

Murder Most Foul at 113

After I retired, I was involved in several unsettling experiences. This was one of the worst.

In 2014, my wife was offered a job to manage a brand-new high rise residential complex in a Brisbane suburb where we lived. This allowed management to always be contactable. Debrena and I moved into the top floor unit and got settled but it was still hectic as workers finished the last of the construction work to the building, which was called Double One Three, after its address number.

Debrena commenced work the following day while I sorted the apartment. She worked 12-hour days seven days a week to fulfill all her duties for this complex. Part of the rental process is a full history check on the people signing the lease. My wife was offered a bonus if all apartments were filled by the end of December. Never issue a challenge to Debrena as she will succeed every time!

As she was working so hard, I was kept the unit clean as well as doing the washing, ironing and cooking dinner each night. It was a great area to live, with everything in walking distance. We both attended the local gym and tried different restaurants and micro-breweries. We also made some wonderful friends who we still keep in contact with today.

Two people applied to rent a one-bedroom ground floor apartment. As usual all checks were carried out.

Nothing negative came back, so they moved in two days later. Marcus said he was a chef, and his girlfriend Mayang was from Indonesia. As part of their lease, they received approval to have two French Bulldogs in their apartment. They were a quiet couple and kept to themselves.

Two weeks after they moved into the apartment, my wife saw Marcus entering the apartment block with a heavily bandaged left arm. She asked him what happened, and he replied he cut his hand at work.

One Saturday, my wife had been working in her office all day, so that afternoon, I asked her if she wanted to go to the Green Beacon Micro Brewing Company then back to a well-known Indian restaurant called the 'Clay Pot.' She agreed so around five, we left our apartment. Arriving on the ground floor, my wife noticed a terrible smell and asked me 'Can you smell that?' I said, 'yes, it smells suspicious. You have to check it out.'

Being the building manager, Debrena had the power to enter any property on site if there is suspected danger to life or property. She knocked a few times and when there was no answer, she used her master key. As she was about to turn the key, Marcus came in the front door carrying two items. He saw my wife and asked, 'what are you doing?' Debrena told him that there was a terrible smell coming from his apartment. Marcus replied, 'I am cooking pigs head broth, and the pot overflowed. Don't worry about it. I will clean it up.'

Alarm bells were ringing in my head by now, thinking all is not right. We watched Marcus open the door ever so slightly and slide around the door and after closing the door we heard the lock applied. The alarm bells in my mind rang again thinking this is very suspicious. I told Debrena that things were not adding up and something was not right.

However, we needed to have dinner, so we left the building. After a few beers at the Green Beacon, we headed up the road to the Clay Pot to have some home cooked Indian food. We arrived home around eight o'clock and switched on the television where I fell asleep on the lounge. A short time later, I awoke when Debrena's work phone rang. It was the assistant Project Manager, who said that Marcus had rung him asking for someone to assist an electrician he had called. The electrician needed to reset the master circuit breaker as the cooking pot had overflowed and shorted the electrical circuit to the unit. With all high-rise apartment buildings, trades people that work within the building need to be registered and a file kept of all their insurances etc.

As Debrena was about to leave, I asked what apartment she was attending. When she said it was Marcus' apartment, I told her, 'I am going with you; something has happened.'

When we arrived, we were met by Marcus and an unknown person who was introduced as the electrician. Debrena asked Marcus what was wrong. He said his cooking pot had shorted the electricity to his apartment, so he called an electrician. Debrena told him he had no right calling a tradesman to attend the building as they need to be approved before being able to work on anything to do with the building operations. Marcus became agitated and started to argue with her even though she explained that it is all stated in the tenant's agreement. At this time, alarm bells were ringing in my head again.

The electrician said, 'lady, I am only here to fix a problem.' So, due to the time of the evening, and not able to leave an occupant with no power, Debrena took him to the electrical sub panel down the hall, asked him if he was sure all was safe to switch on the circuit breaker in the sub panel inside the apartment. He confirmed all was safe.

Marcus asked the electrician how much and he said two hundred and thirty-five dollars. With that Marcus and the electrician proceeded back to his apartment. Debrena then advised Marcus that she needed to enter the apartment to inspect the stove for any damage and safety.

He said, 'No. You have to give me seven days' notice in writing.'

Debrena informed him that as it was a building safety issue, she was able to enter the apartment without any notice as per the current regulations. Marcus argued with her, saying the carpet was wet and he was trying to get some stains out. I got Debrena's attention and pointed to my phone indicating it was on camera as I was sure now that something was wrong.

Marcus entered his apartment, followed by the electrician then Debrena and finally myself. I heard Debrena say, 'My God, Marcus, look at this damage'. As I walked in, the first thing I noticed was how wet the carpets were. Directly on my left was the bathroom but the door was closed. I was so lucky I didn't enter the bathroom.

The next thing we noticed was the damage to the furniture. As I was taking photos, I glanced to my right towards the stove and then a very cold shiver passed through my body. It was like we had entered the middle of an Alfred Hitchcock movie set. I took more photos of a large cooking pot that had boiled its contents over the side and next to the pot was another pot with a strainer with small pieces of cooked meat stuck to it.

By this time Marcus had paid the electrician, and he departed none the wiser. Debrena questioned Marcus about the damage and the state of the place as it was only two weeks old, and everything was brand new, but some of which was damaged beyond repair. I was 99% convinced what had happened now and moved into protection mode, looking after my wife.

Marcus was in a very unstable state and was panicking like you couldn't imagine. I had to place myself between Marcus and my wife for her protection as I couldn't alert her to what we had entered upon. I thought to myself that this called for quick thinking as this could turn for the worse at any second.

I knew Marcus was a black belt and I could see that he was worked up into a frenzy. At any second, he could boil over. In my eyes we both were dealing with a suspected murder, and he would have no hesitation in repeating his actions.

I raised my voice to take control of Marcus and suggested we look into the bedroom as I had seen Mayang's handbag. He said, 'Yes. She forgot it when she left.' I thought that was suspicious because ordinarily, no woman ever forgets her handbag, especially one with their mobile phone sitting on top.

Marcus was pacing backwards and forward. I tried to calm him and said, 'mate we can help you with all this damage and there is no need to worry yourself over this.' I noticed on the side tables beside the bed, dildos and condoms and two tubes of lube.

On leaving the room Marcus was getting very upset and Debrena said, 'I hope you do not do a runner.' I quickly moved in front of him saying 'Marcus there is no need to worry, and we will sort this out Monday. You go and clean up and Debrena and I will leave.' I gave a signal to Debrena to leave. I knew Marcus had knives in his unit and I wasn't sure if he had any other weapons. As we left, I said to Debrena, 'She is cooking in the pot. You must call the Valley Police straight away.' I had taken over a dozen photos and looked back over them while waiting for the police to arrive.

Two uniformed police officers arrived at the front entrance some thirty minutes later and were met by myself and my wife. I produced the photos I had taken. Both of them looked stunned. After some minutes they planned on how they were going to approach Marcus at his unit. Debrena and I moved to the end of the hallway on the ground floor around fifteen meters from the entry to his door. We were positioned just around the end of the hallway so we could look around the corner and clearly see what was happening.

By this time both police officers had knocked on the door without any reply. The senior constable knocked again and after some time I heard the door being unlocked then the door started opening ever so slightly. Marcus appeared through the narrow opening. The Senior Constable asked him if he knew where his partner was. Marcus indicated he did not know. When the Senior Constable told him they would need to enter the unit, he asked if he could have a moment to secure the dogs, which were currently running around inside. The police agreed to this request. Marcus re-entered the unit and locked the door behind him. I knew then this was going to be a serious situation.

Next, I heard Debrena calling me from the rear of the building. She was waving her arms indicating he was in the courtyard of the apartment. I called to both police officers that he was trying to escape out the back. By the time the police officers and I entered the rear alleyway, Marcus had disappeared down the other end. Debrena said she asked him not to run, but he jumped the rear fence and landed within two meters from her with a large knife in his hand before taking off.

The police officers and I set off after Marcus on foot and just as we were turning towards the cross street the Senior Constable's Glock pistol disengaged itself from the holster, rolled on the bitumen and landed hard against my right shin. I was glad the safety was on! By this time backup was called. A search continued for Marcus and involved officers on foot as well as members of the dog squad and plain clothes officers.

We searched under cars and up and down the street, but no trace of Marcus could be found. At this time, no police officer had entered his apartment. Both police officers and I returned to the apartment and met my wife who had a master key that was handed over to the police so they could gain entry. There they found parts of Mayang's dismembered body. Her feet were protruding from a large stockpot which was placed on the floor of the kitchen. Other body parts were found in various garbage bags throughout the unit. Arm bones were found in the dishwasher. It was a nightmare scene.

Some time passed before police located Marcus in a nearby underground carpark with the help of police dogs.

He was found inside an industrial bin with significant injuries to both sides of his throat and wrists. The Queensland Ambulance Service (QAS) was called, but the extent of his injuries meant that he could not be resuscitated.

The next few weeks were a nightmare for us as the investigation and inquest were conducted. The investigation into the circumstances leading to his death was conducted by the Queensland Police Service Ethical Standards Command (ESC) Internal Investigations Group. A separate homicide investigation into the circumstances leading to Mayang's death was conducted by the Fortitude Valley Criminal Investigation Branch.

Marcus' death was reported as a death in custody under the Coroners Act 2003. He died while he was trying to avoid being put into custody. In those circumstances an inquest was mandatory. The focus of the inquest was the actions of the relevant police officers involved in the events leading up to the death of Marcus. Mayang's death was the subject of a separate homicide investigation which concluded that Marcus caused the death.

Statements were tendered by myself and my wife at the inquest. We covered all our dealings with the couple up until the time of their deaths. The police investigation established that Marcus had a mental health history in Victoria, spanning from about 2005. Marcus previously attempted suicide in 2006 when he took an overdose of paracetamol tablets.

Mayang was last seen alive on the third of October 2014. Marcus killed Mayang early that morning by repeatedly stabbing her following a protracted argument. Marcus died from his own actions after inflicting multiple stab wounds to his neck within an industrial bin where he hid after escaping capture.

During the first 24 hours Debrena and I never got a wink of sleep. We were at the police station until four a.m. the next morning giving statements. When we were driven home there was a media frenzy happening with various television stations set up across the road. News reporters were trying to gain entry into the building to get the million-dollar shot of the apartment's front door. They even stooped to offering one shop owner a thousand dollars if he would give them entry into the building.

This incident instantly became international news. Quite a few reports that made the news were incorrect due to people wanting their three minutes of fame. They were desperately trying to contact my wife for an interview and were trying everything to succeed. They were even booking appointments to look at units on site with intentions of renting or buying one. The phone calls to book appointments for an interview had risen by 95%. They were soon filtered out by the staff.

For days the place was like peak hour in the centre of town. Police officers from various branches came and went, the fire service delivered special chemical drums, the clean-up crews did their jobs and on it went.

The office staff were hammered by phone calls of people wanting appointments to see units. Debrena's boss told me to get her out of town for a few days. We flew to Sydney for a few days where we stayed at the famous Rock's region, right under the Sydney Harbour Bridge. We were that tired we could hardly keep our eyes open as our sleep over the past days was very limited. After we collected our luggage, we made our way downstairs to the railway station where we caught a train straight into Circular Key. From there it was only a short walk to the Holiday Inn Hotel in the Rocks. We didn't notice of the room number as we were only looking for a bed to crash. The next morning as we left for breakfast, we caught the lift down to the ground floor. On our return I was opening the unit door and said to my wife 'have a look at the room number'. She said, 'you are kidding!' It was Double One Three '113' the same number as the building back in Brisbane. I thought how strange of a coincidence it was.

Behind the Holiday Inn are various tourist attractions. One is Caminetto Italian Restaurant. I have been going to this restaurant for years and knew the owner well. I spent many a late night there drinking vino with Mario well after the doors closed. I booked a table for the following night for Debrena and myself. When we arrived, I could not believe it, but the table number was Double One Three '113'. Another strange coincidence.

Eight years on now and it just seems like yesterday this incident happened. It has taken its toll on both of us in different ways but our love and support for each other has won the day for us both.

Chapter 17

Let's Break the Stigma

S uffering from a mental health illness is as hard for your loved ones as it is for you.

It took years for me to admit I suffered severe depression and Post-Traumatic Stress Disorder (PTSD). It then took time to seek help as I was embarrassed by what people might think of me. 'Look at him - he is crazy,' or 'don't trust him. He is mad.' I would lose respect and my self-esteem.

Mental illnesses have long been misunderstood and even demonised. People do not fully understand the illness and the people who are suffering are afraid of what people might think of them if they disclose their condition. Given how the mentally ill were treated in the past, this is not an unreasonable fear.

It is an uphill battle to educate people about mental illnesses. Even though the word is out there, it is not fully accepted or understood by the general public as yet. There is still much work to be completed in this area, through talks and media releases, or just getting people to say 'hey, I need to know more about this illness' or admit to themselves they might have a problem and to present themselves for a medical assessment.

Men's mental health is the problem I want to talk about. Men are very stubborn and proud creatures. They will not disclose anything about themselves if it is going to make them look weak or cause embarrassment to themselves. Stigma in this area is such a powerful word and we must break down this word and say, 'hey, its ok to mention you have a mental illness and get support'.

Stigma not only bars men from speaking to their loved ones about mental illness but also from addressing it themselves or seeking help. Several types of stigmas affect men's relationship with mental health, including social stigma, self-stigma, professional and cultural stigma.

The stigma around male mental health is dangerous as men tend to fall into self–destructive behaviours rather than seek professional help.

Men who have no personal experience with depression have more negative views of it in others. Men are more likely to believe people with mental illness are dangerous. Embarrassment and self-stigmatization prevent men from seeking help. Younger men tend to face more stigma about anxiety, depression and suicide.

Some of the most common signs in men suffering from mental illness are: Anger, irritability, or aggressiveness; noticeable changes in mood, energy level, or appetite; difficulty sleeping or sleeping too much; difficulty concentrating, feeling restless, or on edge; increased worry or feeling stressed; misuse of alcohol and other drugs; sadness or hopelessness; suicidal thoughts.

Both men and women can experience depression, but signs and symptoms can be different. Although the primary symptom of depression for many is often a feeling of sadness, men may have a higher tendency than women to feel anger, demonstrate aggressive feelings, and engage in substance abuse.

During my working career I was exposed to many incidents involving serious accidents or death. In my time as a firefighter in the Royal Australian Air Force, I attended both road and aircraft accidents, some of which involved people suffering major trauma and death. Unbeknown to me, this was the start of my mental health problems. Back in the 70's and 80's PTSD was still an illness that was a long way from being understood. And in the military, you were expected to hide any sign of weakness, so you just had to suck it up when you had to deal with these things.

After I discharged from the Air Force, I joined the Brisbane Metropolitan Fire Brigade, now known as the Queensland Fire Department. During those years, I was again exposed to a lot of death and destruction as a front-line firefighter.

The strange thing was that at the time, my mental health issues had not surfaced, and my mind and body were operating as normal. I continued my studies, gained my pilots licence, and then moved into the aviation industry. My life was operating as normal and, knowing what I know now, there were no signs of any mental health problems arising.

It wasn't till the end of my flying career when my flying days were cut short due to needing open-heart surgery that my mental health changed. After my surgery I started having flash backs to incidents I attended and the deceased bodies I handled. I started wondering what was going on and why I was suddenly remembering these things. There is no doubt that open-heart surgery is massively invasive and does change your life for ever.

I have seen so much more destruction and death than most people I know. However, I also see paramedics and doctors who deal with death every day and I think, 'my God, how do they handle it?' Some people seem to be superhuman and they seem to escape the torture of mental illness. However, the truth is that they are suffering in some form from their experiences.

A National Study of Mental Health and Wellbeing released in 2022 reported the facts below. Over two in five Australians aged 16 – 85 years (8.6 million people) had experienced a mental disorder at some time in their life. One in five (4.2 million people) have had a mental disorder lasting a year or more. This goes up to two in five between the ages of 16 – 24 years. Anxiety was the most common group of 12-month mental disorders (about 3.3 million people).

Mental health is a key component of overall health and wellbeing. A mental illness can be defined as a clinically diagnosable disorder that significantly interferes with a person's cognitive, emotional, or social abilities.

The potential for COVID – 19 to impact mental health and well-being was recognised early in the pandemic. In addition to concerns around contracting the virus itself, some of the measures necessary to contain its spread were also likely to negatively impact mental health.

Mental illness affects not just the individual but the wider community as well. The total burden of a disease on a population is defined as the combined loss of years of healthy life due to premature death and living with ill health.

Many things can trigger mental illness in men: relationship problems, financial stress, Covid-19, pressures associated with the workplace, not having productive or paying work, Illness, isolation and drug or alcohol abuse. Even happy events like becoming a father can bring out problems.

Men's mental illness has wide-reaching and profound consequences way beyond the condition itself. Stigma negatively impacts men's mental health and the use of services amid impending disclosures, diminishing social connections, and increasing economic hardship. Past and present times have shown that individuals with mental illness are subject to stigma and treated or thought of less favourably than others due to their mental health challengers. The impacts of stigma can be wide ranging, including access to employment, promotions, housing, social support, health care and more.

One area I believe where a study should be undertaken is men and the different emotional make ups within them. Many males find it difficult to come forward and admit anything that might make them look weak in the eyes of others. However, there is a small group of males that do not follow this regime and do seek out help with suspected mental health issues. There needs to be a study undertaken to find out the differences between this group and others who will not come forward.

After my open-heart operation, I finally spoke to my GP. I told him, 'I am having sweats through the night with vivid dreams of things that happened to me when I was working in front line emergency services.' After a few sessions he referred me to a psychiatrist. I was in two minds as to whether I wanted to go. I felt like I had let myself down, let alone my mother and father. I felt abandoned and hopeless. I was scared as I was only eight weeks post op.

I started reading every book I could get a hold of on mental health. After reading quite a bit on the subject I now see there were very strong pointers towards me suffering some sort of mental illness.

My mind kept saying 'I do not need to see any nut doctor. I will be fine. It's only a short time after the operation. I am tough.' Now what is that telling you? It is a typical answer you would hear from most males because of the way they think.

Being an only child and not having any brother or sisters to confide with made it that much harder. My GP could see I had reservations, and I did not want to go. He explained to me exactly how I felt.

He asked me, 'does your mind feel like there is a tug of war going on inside? With one section saying yes go and the other section saying no, don't go, you are tougher than that?' I agreed, 'yes, that is what I am feeling.' He told me, 'Be the tougher man and say to yourself - I need help - and go.' So, I did.

After my first session with the psychiatrist, I felt a load had been taken off my shoulders - a load I never knew was there. I went once a week and began to dive deeper into my mind and understand the reason I was diagnosed with PTSD and severe depression.

My psychiatrist said I have had the symptoms for years, but it took the open-heart operation to bring the illness to the surface. He said, 'people can go around for years and one day something will trigger something inside your body and the illness will surface. For other people who are confronted with trauma it can affect them immediately.'

So now I take regular medication to control my condition. I would rather call the illness a condition as it sounds much better. Just my personal thoughts.

I certainly still have my ups and downs and sometimes it is very hard to handle. However, I have a wonderful support group IN my wife and my close friends from the military who also suffer mental conditions.

I have read many books to try and understand my condition and how I can handle it better. I have learned to accept that it will be with me for life.

I was embarrassed at first about telling anyone but after a while I remembered that word STIGMA. I was no longer going to hide by pretending I did not suffer a mental illness.

I think the best thing you can recognise are the triggers that can set your condition off: ambulance sirens, helicopters flying over, crowded, noisy or confined areas, driving a car, running late for an appointment, watching the news reports etc. You need to recognise these triggers as it is the first step to recovery. With a mental health condition, everyone is different in how they handle the condition and what triggers set them off. You will have to take notes to start with to find out.

The next thing is you must admit to yourself that you have this condition for life. It is up to you to control how you feel and when you feel it coming on. If you wake up one morning feeling like shit, do something about it. Stay home in bed all day or if it comes on at the shopping centre, leave and go home to a quiet area of the house and relax. Let a member of your family know how you are feeling and let them help you if they offer. When my condition takes hold, it can last from a day up to two weeks at its worst.

I recently had surgery with two procedures in two days involving general anaesthesia. Three days later this sent me into a major depression. I feel like I am fighting my mind, and the tug of war has started again making me feel like crap. I have been to my doctor who asked me if I felt suicidal, which I replied no, (and please be honest with yourself, remember you are not the only one suffering in your family). He knows me well enough now to allow me to monitor myself for a few days where it was agreed if I get much worse, I am to report to a hospital. If it is still the same after 4 days, I can increase my medication till I am back to some normality.

Remember you are not alone and do not ever think that. There are plenty of experienced people out there who are trained to help you. Everyone that has this condition handles it differently. However, acceptance is the big rule here.

I find keeping myself occupied in my day-to-day life is a must. I have a number of interests I am involved with including giving back to the mental health industry as an ambassador for Black Dog Institute and the Australia and New Zealand Mental Health Association. I am also keeping fit as my condition is controlled on how my body is treated. I eat healthy and watch my weight.

You also need to become connected with a mental health association so you can talk to people in general and have friends who understand in more detail what you are going through. You never know, you might just make some lifelong friends.

Remember you cannot burn the candle at both ends and your body needs rest. Also watch your alcohol intake if you are on medication. Take your medication as prescribed unless you have the doctor's permission to vary the dose. Watch comedy movies, listen to upbeat music, let your partner or family know how you feel and when you are on a downward slide. Do something straight away to stop the slide and seek medical help. Have some close friends who understand your condition and who you can call on.

Value yourself. Treat yourself with kindness and respect. Make time for your hobbies and favourite projects. Learn another language, learn to play an instrument.

Respecting oneself is very important. You have to come to peace with yourself. Avoid self-criticism. This will never help you come to terms with your condition.

Be around positive people. The facts are if you want to get rich you are not going to hang around gamblers, you are going to hang around wealthy people. In this case you are going to hang around positive people, people that want to succeed in life.

Learn how to deal with stress, learn about time out and quiet time. Most importantly set realistic goals for yourself.

I find what works for me is being around positive people because you can feel the positivity in the air. Set your goals and become an achiever in your life. Volunteer your time in helping others and pass on your knowledge. Be prepared for setbacks as they will happen. However, you have fought the battle, and you know what works for you, and you will win.

Remember that life is full of battles. It is nothing special to come across issues or jobs you cannot solve. Remember the term "team effort" - a mental condition needs a team effort to help anyone get back to a normal lifestyle. It cannot be completed alone.

Look at your previous lifestyle. It might need changing - less alcohol, more sleep, better nutrition and yes, you guessed it, more water. I drink a minimum of three litres a day now and it has made a world of difference in my general health.

I can go on saying do this and do that. However, I will not kid you, it is not easy to change your habits. You must want to do it and be truthful with yourself. It is bloody hard. The only thing I can say is start slowly and build up over time.

In life, where there is a positive, there will always be a negative. I am not here to point out what positives or negatives there might be. That's up to you to work out. But I am here to say – it can be done. You can do this.

Chapter 18

Adventures before Dementia

The last six years have been momentous in Australia: Bushfires occurred from late 2019 to mid-2020 in every state and territory, destroying 2600 homes and killing 34 people. The ACT became the first Australian region to legalise recreational cannabis. Australia suffered lockdowns and social restrictions due to the Covid – 19 pandemics. In the 2022 Australian federal election Anthony Albanese defeated Scott Morrison to become the 31st Prime Minister of Australia and the first labour government in eight years. Queen Elizabeth the second died aged 96, after a reign of 70 years.

During 2019 our preparations were under way for Debrena to finally retire. We purchased a Mazda BT 50 GT the previous year and had it fitted out with all the required off-road gear, including a long-range tank, onboard compressor, lift kit and much more as we were planning to spend a lot of time off road. We also purchased a near new single axle fully off-road caravan. As September approached, we were both eagerly putting together everything we thought we needed for four to five years on the road.

Being avid nature lovers and having a great respect for our Australian native animals, we both founded Endangered Species Supporters Australia (ESSA) in 2018.

After our official launch on ABC radio in Broken Hill in September 2019 it attracted a strong following. We spoke to various groups around Australia about the sad fact that Australia has the highest number of endangered or extinct animals of any country in the world. Only we Australians can help reduce these numbers and save our native animals from extinction. It has been a great success and I was awarded an Australia Day Medallion in 2020 for services to wildlife.

Another award I received in 2020 was an Honorary Life Membership in the Australian Parachute Federation. It was a wonderful surprise.

The bushfires put a halt to our travels and our wildlife program. We had to change our plans and head to South Australia to continue. We ended up assisting on Kangaroo Island during the fires and spent time with Blaze Aid. The destruction and devastation that was caused on Kangaroo Island by the bush fires had to be seen to fully understand.

I helped one poor family that lost everything including their two homes, their stock, their sheds, just everything bar the shirts on their backs. They were in their eighties and the farmer's wife was on her second bout of cancer. They lived in the old shearing sheds amongst the rubbish. They slept on a mattress on the concrete with old blankets to keep them warm. As soon as I saw this, I spoke to a friend in Canberra and before long a portable hut was sent to the farm. No one in Australia today should be subjected to conditions like these people were enduring.

My wife and I also spent five months on Flinders Island off the North of Tasmania delivering 300 baby Angus calves. The farmer who was based in Yass New

South Wales could not leave NSW due to the Covid – 19 lockdown requirements. So, he advertised, and we were lucky enough to be given the chance to help out. We learnt so much about cattle and especially the Angus breed.

Our best time was spent up at "Angorichina Station" in the North Flinders Rangers in Northern South Australia - 180,000 acres of pure splendid Australian outback beauty. We are such good friends now Ian, Di, Ed and Alice and their two children Eloise and Jimmy. We repaired buildings and shearing sheds; I plastered ceilings, and we painted walls and connected water supplies. I also went shooting for food for the sheep dogs and setting traps for the dingoes. This was not easy work.

A gentleman from the Eyre Peninsular was paid by the SA government to go around the properties and teach the farmers how to set dingo traps properly. They should make a TV series about this true outback legend. He was known as "Gonzo the Bare Foot Bushman". He never wore boots and walked barefoot through the biggest thorns you would ever see in the Australian outback. The soles of his feet were like steel. In the back of his four-wheel drive, he had a large fridge where the pub was open anytime of the day.

It was in September 2020 I found out I had contracted cancer for a second time, but this didn't deter us from our planned adventure around Australia. It meant we would be based in Adelaide, which by chance was the best move we could have made.

We stayed at the caravan park right on Brighton beach south of Adelaide during my treatments. The coming months involved plenty of trips to various doctors until they decided what course of action to take.

The day of the operation Debrena drove me to the hospital at Ashford. Due to Covid-19 restrictions she was not allowed in the hospital, so it was hard saying goodbye in the car out front. As I entered the hospital, I was embarking on a road untravelled. The unknown can be scary, but I have been in other difficult situations before, and I thought that this was no different.

As I was prepared for surgery, I kept my breathing at a slow pace because there is no need to panic. That would only make things worse for myself. It was not easy and took all of my self-control to keep myself focused. My surgeon went through a few final details. Dr Jimmy Eteuati was the most incredible gentleman you would ever meet.

Next the anaesthetist appeared, placed a cannula in my arm and asked me to walk into the theatre. Having had plenty of surgeries before, walking into an operating theatre is the least of my worries. The anaesthetist said he was going to place a nerve block in my back. I could feel the injection, then I was asked to lay down on the operating table. My eyes became heavy and that was it. I woke up four hours later heavily sedated in intensive care. I was told they had removed 850 mm of my small bowel, and the operation was a success.

Debrena was unable to visit me, but I was under heavy sedation, so the first few days flew by. I had a few setbacks but was on the road to recovery. Unfortunately, I had been taken off all of my regular medication and I wasn't feeling well in my mind. At this stage with everything going on I never realised that my regular medication involving my PTSD and depression drugs had not been readministered. I was becoming very depressed with bad thoughts entering my head.

It is a road I have been down before and read a lot about, so understanding and knowing my state of mind was paramount. You can never say, 'it will be alright,' because quite simply it won't be. I was struggling hard with my feelings and battling with my pain and everything that happened previously. I looked up at the television and the way it was mounted on the wall stand. I realised that if I removed the sheet and tied it off it would be an easy way to hang myself. Luckily, I knew it was time to let the hospital staff know that my thoughts were going way off track, and I was entertaining suicidal thoughts.

I was able to admit to myself I could no longer handle the situation I was in and needed help. I was not brave or embarrassing myself. I was admitting to myself I needed help, otherwise I could have taken my life that day.

The problem with suicide is that it doesn't end there. I have a wife and family who would be affected and great friends too. It's not always about one person, so I ask everyone reading this book to seek help if times become hard because there is a no return. When you enter the slide, the deeper you fall the less grip you have to return to normality. Eventually I believe you can reach a stage of no return. I almost reached that stage on that day but realised I still had a choice, and I chose to get help. Otherwise, I probably would not be here today.

It wasn't long till I was released from hospital, and I was back in the fresh sea air of Brighton Beach. My recovery took some months and as Christmas was approaching, the family planned to meet in a house by the Tamar River at Beauty Point north of Launceston. After my brush with death again, I was looking forward to having a wonderful Christmas and we did.

Our next adventure was into the Northern Territory. We travelled to Woomera, then via the Oodnadatta Track to William Creek. We visited Lake Eyre then drove back to Marla on the Stuart Highway just south of the NT border.

The three weeks on the track were spectacular. The creeks were abundant with native Australian wildlife. The farmers were so accommodating and the tranquillity of being alone in the middle of the outback was surreal.

The outback is a picturesque part of Australia, but it can turn on you at any time causing life threatening situations. In my time in the U.S. I was trained in battlefield medicine and so my medical kit was fitted out with a defibrillator, intravenous cannulas, intravenous painkillers, green whistles, complete sutures kits, antibiotics, bacitracin, Lidocaine injections, bags of 500 mm and one litre saline bags, special bandages and much more. I also had a military HF radio with connections to Royal Flying Doctor Bases around Australia. The radio could plot our track and give our location in real time on our website.

We arrived in Marla after three weeks. We refuelled our car and topped up our gas and spare fuel drums. We had a late breakfast at the roadhouse before heading north over the NT border to the Kulgera Roadhouse. We met the new owners, and they convinced us to stay, which wasn't hard because we loved the area and meeting new people.

We were offered free accommodation, food and drinks in return for our help. It was a completely different life, and we thoroughly enjoyed every minute we were there. We met some fantastic people who like us loved the outback life and decided to stay for a few weeks or months like Ryan the mad Englishman, Mike and Kara, Sophie and

Seb, the owners May and Fong and many more people. We helped with the chores from plumbing to chopping mulga wood for the fire each night during the cold winter.

Our local rubbish tip was situated some 5 km east of the roadhouse near the Ghan Railway line from Adelaide to Darwin. Being a wild boy, I noticed there were plenty of disused gas bottles lying beside the tip. One afternoon when things were quiet and Ryan and I had finished cutting a truck load of timber I said, 'let's go to the tip and I'll show you a proper explosion.'

I rigged up three 20kg gas bottles, lit a fire and ran for cover. Soon enough there was a massive explosion and the fire ball that erupted was amazing. We had some great fun at the tip in Kulgera.

Our trips to Alice Springs were another story. It was a leisurely 3-hour drive along the Stuart highway via the Pine Gap turnoff. We went to the Alice about once a fortnight to collect supplies, including all the alcohol for the hotel side of the operation, extra food and any work materials we needed.

Ryan or Seb came with me, and it was a full day as we used to leave before sunup and arrive back well after dark. As we knew the local police officer in town, we used to push the throttle a little bit harder to the floor, saving over an hour travelling time.

The next police station was at Uluru about four hours west of us, then there were the Alice police who would patrol south of Alice just to the city limits, so we slowed down about five km from the city limits. We always found time to go to the Diplomat Hotel for a good steak lunch, plus a few beers and bets.

The Kulgera Roadhouse is the closest hotel and pub to the geographical centre of Australia. The nearest Aboriginal community is at the Finke River to the east.

In August 2022 I drove to Uluru, where I arranged to leave my vehicle at the local police station. I was driven to the airport in the police car to catch my flight to Brisbane then onto Adelaide where I met Debrena, and our Air Force friends Keran and Glenys and Sandy and Pat for our three yearly RAAF Firefighters reunion. Being early August, it was cold and raining.

While I was in Adelaide, I had my regular cancer scan to check everything was going as planned.

After the weekend of festivities, Debrena and I flew to Melbourne with a connecting flight to Darwin. We spent a few days in Darwin before travelling over to Bali for a few weeks. During our stay in Darwin, I booked a few tours out to Kakadu for Debrena and I which we enjoyed very much.

The day before we left for Bali, I received a phone call from my cancer specialist indicating my cancer had returned and I needed further treatment. It wasn't a shock. It was just an issue we had to deal with as soon as possible after our return from Bali.

How a person initially deals with something of high importance is very important. I didn't panic. I just said to myself *be strong and we will win this battle as well*. It's never easy for the family and this has to be taken into account by the way you handle things during these times of uncertainty.

On our return from Bali, we flew to Darwin then a few days later onto Sydney before catching a connecting flight back to Uluru. Then we had a 3-hour drive back to Kulgera.

We broke the bad news to everyone that we had to return to Adelaide for further treatment. After leaving Kulgera for the long trip south we stopped at the outback town of Woomera.

Following the advances in military technology of World War 11, Australia and the United Kingdom formed the Anglo-Australia Joint Project in 1946. The centrepiece of the project was the establishment of a long-range weapons testing facility at Woomera. The area was declared a Prohibited Area in 1947, and the first military trial took place in December 1947.

From 1957, Woomera became a global focal point for space activity, including being chosen as the launch point for the European Launcher Development Organisation (ELDO) At the height of its space activity, Woomera had the second highest number of rockets launches in the world after NASA's Facilities at Cape Canaveral in Florida.

During my operations as a Gulfstream pilot contracted to NASA, I witnessed a number of rocket launches including five Shuttle launches. I was living in Cocoa Beach, Florida and in a perfect position to wander from the back yard down to the beach and watch the launches. If the launch times were right, I would call everyone around for a few drinks and a barbecue of ribs and hamburgers. Sometimes the get-togethers went well into the night. It was a tradition.

There were five shuttles - Columbia, Challenger, Discovery, Atlantis, and Endeavour. There were 135 launches at a cost of $196 billion, a mere hundred billion over the original estimated cost. A total of 355 astronauts flew in the shuttle and there were fourteen deaths (seven in Columbia in 2003, seven in Challenger in 1986). The cumulative time in space was three years, 221 days 19 hours, during which 20, 958 orbits of the earth were made for a total distance travelled of 543 million miles.

My good friend Commanding Officer Squadron Leader Anthony Roe of the Royal Australian Airforce 20 Squadron based at Woomera asked me to call in for a few days. Those days were very special.

Anthony and his wife Simone met us at our caravan and drove us back to the Stuart Highway near Spud's Roadhouse. We turned south along the highway for about one km before turning off on a dirt road. As we continued down this rough track, we saw a massive lake known as the Island Lagoon in the distance. Down in the valley stood an abandoned site of massive old buildings surrounded by a double wire fence that was separated by what looked like no man's land. There were still two radar domes left. I asked Anthony, 'what was this place?' He told me it was called Nurrungar and was a base run by the ADF and the US Air Force from 1969 to 1999.

As I unlocked the gate to the secure area I could sense a feeling of history, a sense of how top secret this place must have been not that long ago. As I stepped inside the main building I was told about the layout of the building and what went on in every room. I felt a cold shiver go through my body like I had seen a ghost. It had only closed its doors 25 years before. I was shown how the communications could not be tracked by outside sources and much more.

I was taken into a room that looked like launch control in Cape Canaveral. On the wall was a massive drawing of the Space Shuttle flying over a map of Australia. I was totally in awe. Although the shuttle was controlled in America, there was a dead zone where they could lose contact. There had to be a backup if communications were lost, and Woomera was one of the places that provided that backup. I was told this room was the backup for any problem that might have happened in America. In other words, this was Cape Canaveral two. It was the hub of controlling the Space Shuttle if anything failed in America.

I thought about that, how this complex sits in the middle of the outback a few kilometres off a main highway where people travelling up north or down south pass by the unmarked road without a second thought. But what was in there was amazing.

After treatments in Adelaide, we returned home to Brisbane in early 2023 and continued treatment for my cancer. My wife and I plan to fully renovate our house on Macleay Island. I have started extending the large deck on the rear of the house and replacing the roof on both the house and the main three bay shed. I have a good friend Darren across the road who helps me with the major work. Nothing is ever too much trouble for Darren. Darren and his daughter Ebony are the best neighbours you could ever wish for.

We also own a house near the mouth of the Tamar River opposite Beauty Point in Tasmania. It was here we met a wonderful couple Brant and Rachel Webb who have become great friends. Brant, you will remember was one of the survivors of the Beaconsfield Mine Disaster. Brant and

I have had some memorable times together as we both love fishing.

In February 2023 my wife and I travelled for six weeks throughout Asia where we visited Vietnam, Cambodia, Thailand, Malaysia, and Singapore. It was a wonderful holiday showing my wife the places I had travelled too previously.

When we flew into old Saigon, now known as Ho Chi Min city, I revisited the battlefield of Long Tan to pay my respects to the Australians who fought a bloody battle there during the Vietnam War.

In August 2023 Debrena and I travelled to Japan for two weeks. We spent a night in Tokyo before travelling on the bullet train to Osaka. We spent a few days visiting the sites of Osaka as well as attending a cooking class. As we travel the world, we love food and plan a cooking class in most of the countries we visit.

We also caught the bullet train to Hiroshima and visited the site where the atomic bomb was dropped. Needless to say, it is a very moving place.

On our return to Tokyo, we stopped at the large lake near Mt Fuji. I convinced Debrena to go on one of the most amazing roller coaster rides in the world. It still holds the Guiness World Record. It actually pulls 3.5 Gs in the turns and the experience is out of this world. We took a bike ride around the lake and visited a traditional Japanese restaurant where we experienced the wonderful food Japan has to offer and Debrena experienced Sake for the first time. I couldn't get over how the cost of living in Japan was much cheaper than Australia compared to a number of years before when I last visited.

In October 2023 we returned to Bangkok in Thailand before flying onto Helsinki in Finland. From there we flew up into the Arctic Circle to a town called Rovaniemi. Rovaniemi is the capital of Lapland and the official hometown of Santa Claus. When we left Bangkok, it was 35 degrees and 15 hours later when we arrived in Rovaniemi it was – 15 degrees and snowing.

Lapland is Finland's northernmost region, a sparsely populated area bordering Sweden, Norway, Russia and the Baltic Sea. It's known for its vast subarctic wilderness, ski resorts and natural phenomena including the midnight sun and the Northern Lights. After spending four nights in Rovaniemi around -15 degrees C we caught the Santa Claus Express train back to Helsinki for a few days then crossed the Gulf of Finland to visit Estonia.

After that, we flew to London for a week. The Fin-Air aircraft was running late, and we needed to be in London as I bought tickets to the "Tina Turner Musical" in London's West End for Debrena's birthday. I said to the driver we needed to be at the Aldwych Theatre by 1930 hrs. That gave us 45 minutes in peak hour traffic and raining. We arrived outside the Theatre just five minutes late, an amazing feat by the English driver. Tina delivered an unforgettable show that highlighted both her indomitable spirit and phenomenal talent. The musical was a powerhouse of emotions, and Tina's voice is still exceptional. Her fiery energy on stage was absolutely unstoppable, leaving the audience in awe. It's true, there is only one Tina.

After visiting the sights of London, we caught the Euro Rail train under the English Channel and visited France, Netherlands, Germany, the Czech Republic and Austria before flying to Istanbul, Turkey. From there we boarded the Norwegian Cruise Liner "Norwegian Dawn" and travelled the Mediterranean visiting the Turkish Riviera. We were supposed to visit Tel Aviv and Haifa in Israel. However, due to rising tensions in the region the ship bypassed these towns and next stopped at Egyptian Port of Alexandria. From there we visited Cairo including Giza's colossal Pyramids and the Great Sphinx.

From Alexandria the ship travelled to the Suez Canal then into the Red Sea. On the way we visited Sharm el-Sheikh at the bottom of the Sinai Peninsula then on to Aqaba in Jordan before overnighting in Safaga in Egypt. We then went east to Jeddah in Saudi Arabia before spending the next four days at sea.

When my wife and I boarded the Norwegian Dawn in Istanbul Turkey we were onboard before lunchtime. We always liked to board the ships early as that gave us time to explore the ship before many people arrived.

That afternoon we proceeded to the "wine bar" situated just aft of midships on level 7. It was here we met a group of American gentlemen who were widely travelled and loved fine wine. From that day forth we met at the bar every evening. On the second night the ships General Manager Alain joined us and became part of our unofficial "Wine Club" as it became known. A great group of people with many friendships made.

The cruise Director Jerry joined us and asked me to be a guest speaker in the auditorium. I said I would be delighted. The size of the crowd surprised me and it was an honour to be asked to give that talk.

My biggest surprise came when I received an email in 2024 from the Governor General's office in Canberra asking me if I would accept an "Order of Australia". I was totally blown away and said yes!

I have donated a lot of my time in helping others in the world over the past decades. I am an Australian Ambassador for the Australia Day Council as well as being an Australian Ambassador for Bravery Trust, White Ribbon, Black Dog Institute and Australia and New Zealand Mental Health Association which keeps me very busy.

I have many plans I want to put into place as soon as I shake the cancer problem, and my health is better. Over the next few years, I would like to walk the Kokoda Track, do the base camp at Mt Everest, break the world height record for a tandem parachute jump and raise money by doing these adventures for a number of charities to help others less fortunate.

In May of 2024 Debrena and I travelled to a remote part of Vanuatu and stopped in a village for four weeks at a small community called Emua. Emua is situated just over one hours drive north of the capital Port Vila on the main island of Efate. On our arrival into Port Vila via a Virgin Airlines flight from Brisbane Australia direct to Vanuatu we were met by the owner of the hut where we were staying. His name was Kenneth, and he was holding my name up on a piece of carbuard. As soon as we shook hands, I could see this bright smile appear on his face. It was the way of all Ni-Vanuatu people. They are such a happy group.

It was my tenth time to this enchanting country. The weather was mild and after our bags were packed into Kenneth's cousin's van, we were off to the shopping centre to collect some supplies. One of the supplies was a cold carton of the local brew "Tusker".

As we departed Port Vila heading north it was noticeable that the roads were in need of some serious repair. As we headed up the steep mountain, the view back over to Port Vila was magnificent.

A few months earlier, I contacted the Vanuatu High Commission in Canberra offering my services as an official delegate for Vanuatu in Queensland. I received a reply saying they had recently advertised a position for a Consul General to be based in Brisbane, so I applied for this position.

Just before we departed Australia for Vanuatu, I was told the position was now called a "Trade Commissioner" and I was asked to reapply if I was still interested. On my arrival at the Foreign Affairs Department, I wanted the job so much that I was as nervous as a school child fronting the principal. The director advised me all my security clearances were in order, the official paperwork would be drawn up and I would be sworn in by the Deputy Prime Minister. I was happy in many ways. Vanuatu is a country that is close to my heart, especially having been married there. It meant so much to me to be their Trade Commissioner for Queensland.

Over the coming weeks with meetings and touring the island I came up with a plan to improve a number of items and services. This is one of the better challenges I have given myself over the past years and I am determined to succeed.

By this time Debrena and I were given hellos and smiles everywhere we walked throughout Emua village. We were slowly learning the local language, Bislama. The community soon heard about this by what they call the "coconut telephone" and the respect we received was overwhelming. After the community members were advised of my new appointment I had Rock Star status.

I met with the Deputy Prime Minister and the Director General of Foreign Affairs a few times to discuss my role and talk to them about the improvements I wanted to make. After I explained my ideas, they agreed I could proceed.

I had a number of meetings with the Chief and Chairman from the Emua community and talked about the plans I had for the community and how we could use the community as an exhibit to other communities. Emua is the main community that services several large Islands to the North of the main Island of Efate. In total Efate services around 5,000 plus Ni-Vanuatu residences.

Health is a major problem facing the people of Vanuatu. Having already spent one week in Emua Community I experienced a medical emergency one night around 23.30 hours. It got that bad by 0230 hrs the next morning Debrena had to call the Port Vila ambulance. My pain was 10/10 and was in need of strong medication to ease the pain. By 0630hrs I could hear the ambulance coming down the track. By 0700hrs The Paramedics injected me with a shot of morphine. After about 15 mins the pain started to subside. I was then directed to the ambulance and driven to Port Vila public hospital. This was another experience that I found confronting.

I was placed on a bed in a room with 10 beds and given more morphine over the next 3 hours along with an ultrasound. I was discharged later that day and given a script for morphine tablets. I called into every chemist in Port Vila, and they said they hadn't had this drug for four months. The strongest drug they could sell me was Ibuprofen. This did nothing for me but over the next two days it settled down and I continued my time in this wonderful part of the South Pacific.

Football is the major sport played by all the males within Vanuatu. Their league is very competitive, and they are aligned with FIFA. Vanuatu has two very good players one who plays for the Mariners in New South Wales and the other is playing for Wellington in New Zealand. Both teams are part of the A-League competition held in Australia and New Zealand.

I am holding talks soon with the Brisbane Roar, a team that has seen great success in the league over the years. I would like the Roar to set up a football school where young people could learn skills and hopefully be part of the league in Australia or overseas.

I am also looking at extending the small wharf at Emua another 40 meters so more boats can arrive under safer conditions. When the weather becomes extreme it is impossible to transport people from their home islands to Emua. A suitable rescue boat is needed to transport the sick and injured to Emua wharf because at the moment there is nothing.

I am also working for an ambulance to be stationed at the First Aid post that services a number of communities around the area. Right now, there is no trained nurse or doctor on site. They have a first aid lady, and an old troop carrier set up as an ambulance. The strongest medicine you can receive is Panadol. My aim is to have a proper fully equipped ambulance set up with a driver and a paramedic on station.

I have also had meetings with the Port Vila Lord Mayor about the logistics of getting two compact garbage trucks sent to Vanuatu with a number of recycling bins to trial a rubbish collection and start a "Clean up Vanuatu" theme.

Vanuatu is quiet a clean place however there is more needed to keep the islands in pristine condition.

Vanuatu is very rich in export products. There is a wide variety of items from seafood to coconut oil that is waiting to be sold to overseas countries.

My position as "Trade Commissioner" is not an easy one by any means, however I always liked a challenge in life and most of all to help people. As I mentioned before, their health is my paramount concern and seeking assistance in this area is not easy and each task will take time. I have found that when aid is given, the items are put into operation until something happens, such as a break down. If there are no spare parts or experience to repair the item, this renders the equipment useless.

My idea and let us use the resurfacing of the roads as an example. I seek out a company who has the correct machinery and it is transported over to Vanuatu, everything that is needed to carry out a road resurfacing task is on hand. Training for all the road surfacing crews is paramount so that when break downs happen, the machinery doesn't end up being unusable.

I have a meeting with the Redland City Council where I will present an offer to Mayor Jos Mitchell and her councillors to form a sister city agreement with Port Vila in Vanuatu.

I think the future for Vanuatu is a bright one. Vanuatu was badly destroyed by two cyclones last year and more recently the earthquake that damaged many buildings in Port Vila the capital. The country is still recovering from the force of mother nature. With the assistance of their close neighbours, I am certain this magnificent country will recover fully and be enjoyed by anyone that arrives upon her shores.

The highlight of 2024 was when I was honoured to receive an OAM or Order of Australia Medal for my life's work.

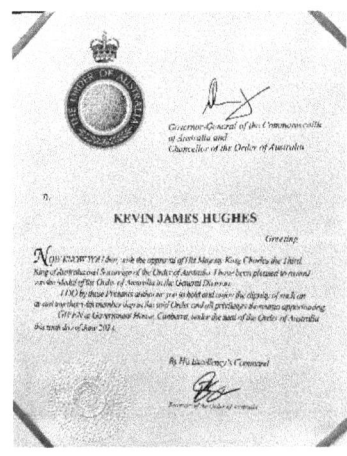

With the former Governor- General Dame Quentin Bryce
AD,CVO

With Former Governor-General, Sir Peter Cosgrove
AK,CVO,MC (ret'd)

*With the Governor-General her Excellency the
Honourable Ms Sam Mostyn AC*

Age is just a number and with many injuries I carry it could have stopped me in my tracks, however I am a fighter and never give up. Remember if you stop using it, you lose it.

This year in 2025 Debrena and I are travelling to Cairns and Cooktown where I will be presenting awards on Australia Day as Australia Day Ambassador then mid-February we are travelling with friends on another South Pacific cruise, come March we are back to Bali before travelling to Palau for two weeks. In April we are off to the Cook Islands. August sees us travelling to Alaska, Canada and the USA. My schedule in between trips will entail at least 4 trips to Vanuatu as Trade Commissioner.

As you have read mental health is very close to my heart and everyone needs to tackle this issue affecting so many people in the world head on. I will leave you with this final thought.

Mental health includes our emotional, psychological, and social well-being. It affects how we think, feel, and act. It also helps determine how we handle stress, relate to others, and make healthy choices. Mental health is important at every stage of our life, from childhood to adolescence then through adulthood. I beg everyone reading this book, if you have any signs, please speak to somebody or seek medical help. If you know anyone that suffers, lend them a shoulder and talk to them. **You might save a life.**